Dynamic People Skills

Dynamic People Skills

Dexter Yager
Yager *with* Ron Ball

Published by InterNET Services Corporation
USA

Edited by Susan Frederick

Cover photos by Mike Carroll

Project management by Valerie Munei

© 1997 by InterNET Services Corporation
All rights reserved

Printed in the United States of America

17 16
32

This Book Can Change Your Life!

Often when reading a book, we fully decide to apply what we need to our lives. All too often though, we forget our good intentions. Here are five practical ways to turn good intentions into practical habits.

1. **READ THIS BOOK MORE THAN ONCE.** Let me encourage you to personalize and internalize these principles. Many people have generated a turning point in their lives by reading this book from cover to cover and then reading it at least once again.

2. **UNDERLINE AND MAKE NOTES.** Have a pen and a highlighter in your hand. Underline specific lines and paragraphs—a simple act that will triple your retention rate. Write your own thoughts in the margins and make it your book.

3. **REREAD YOUR UNDERLINES.** By underlining and high-lighting, you can quickly review key items and portions of this book. Then reread your key items over and over.

4. **APPLY THE MATERIAL IMMEDIATELY.** There is an old saying, "Hear something... you forget it. See something... you remember it. Do something... you understand it. Apply what you learn as soon as you possibly can... it helps you understand and remember it."

5. **PRIORITIZE WHAT YOU WANT TO LEARN.** Select two or three principles from this book. Apply them faithfully, and make them a habit.

Remember, every person alive struggles with turning good intentions into habits. Using these five points will turn wishing into doing and doing into habits.

As I mentioned earlier, many successful people in the past have traced a new, exciting, profitable chapter in their lives to the reading of a specific book. I want that to happen to you!

Write the date you start reading this book:

_____

May the date you have just written be the beginning of incredible blessings, rewards, and growth!

Dexter R. Yager, Sr.

CONTENTS

ABOUT THE AUTHORS *ix*

PROLOGUE *xi*

INTRODUCTION:
The Key to Success in Life *xvii*

PART **One**
Developing Dynamic Relationships *1*
1   Situations Change When You Change *3*
2   Positive Patterns for Success *21*
3   Moving Forward with People *35*
4   How to Stay Motivated Forever *53*

PART **Two**
Knocking Out Negatives That Spoil Your
Relationships *67*
5   Deal with Regret *69*
6   Overcome Rejection *81*
7   Get a Grip on Your Ego *95*
8   Eliminate Negative Patterns *103*

PART **Three**
Understanding Who You Are *115*
9   Choosing Your View of Human Nature *117*
10   Emotions and How They Work *127*

PART **Four**
Building a Powerful Marriage *141*
11   Looking for a Life Partner *143*
12   Keys to a Fulfilling Marriage *157*

CONCLUSION:
You Can Do It! *171*

EPILOGUE *175*

PEOPLE SKILLS REFERENCE *179*

ABOUT THE AUTHORS

Dexter Yager is considered one of America's most influential and successful business leaders. A millionaire many times over, he owns and operates over three dozen corporations/partnerships worldwide and has developed the largest distributor organization of its kind, which includes hundreds of thousands of businesspeople throughout the world. As a popular speaker, consultant, and motivator, he spends a great deal of time with people: counseling individuals, consulting with small groups, and addressing large conventions all over the world. Being a husband to his wife, Birdie, for thirty-nine years, a father of seven children, and a grandfather to over fifteen grandchildren, Dexter realizes the importance of teaching commonsense people skills as well as sound business, spiritual, and financial principles.

Dexter received the Bicentennial Award for the Most Outstanding Christian Businessman in 1976, the Humanitarian Award at the Washington Charity Awards Dinner in 1985, and an honorary doctorate degree in business administration from Southwest Baptist University in 1996. He has been a guest on many television talk shows and has been featured in several national magazines and books. He has also authored eleven best-selling books, including *Everything I Know at the Top I Learned at the Bottom* and the million-copy best-seller *Don't Let Anybody Steal Your Dream.*

Ron Ball, president of his own corporation, is a noted speaker and author who has addressed thousands of people at business conventions, civic rallies, and Christian crusades in America, Europe, Australia, and Asia. He has also appeared on television and radio broadcasts in forty states.

Ron graduated with a bachelor of arts from Asbury College and holds a master of divinity from Asbury Theological Seminary. He also received the Financial Researcher of the Year award from the Financial Research Institute of America in 1990. Ron has authored *Successful Family Ties* and has coauthored several books with Dexter Yager, including *Ordinary Men, Extraordinary Heroes*; *A Millionaire's Common-Sense Approach to Wealth*; and *The Mark of a Millionaire.* He has also recorded over two hundred audiocassettes, including the best-selling *Practical Steps to Financial Freedom, How to Grow a Business, Positive Family Principles, Bull's-Eye Living,* and *Stress Surpassed.*

Some people see my dad as a controversial figure. Others say
that controversial is the last phrase they'd apply to him.
These are people whose lives have been deeply affected by
Dexter Yager. When they talk about him, they smile. Some
of them talk about him through their tears. For those of us
who know Dexter, there is no controversy. Dexter knows
people. He understands them and he loves them. No one
who knows him could doubt that.

In fact, over the last three decades he's changed more lives
than anyone else I know of. He's taught success to thousands
of people, many of whom have taken his words to heart and
taken the initiative to bring that success into their own lives.

Consistency of principle, relentless belief in people,
a commitment of faith, a special kind of tenderness and love,
down-to-earth wisdom, and those dancing blue eyes that
seem to take in everything are what people who know him
think of when they say "Dexter Yager."

As I worked on this book, it occurred to me that many of
you who read it won't have the privilege of knowing my
dad personally. Maybe you've heard him speak on a tape

or at a large meeting. Maybe you've just heard of him. Whatever caused you to pick up this book, I hope you'll know him a little better when you're through with it. Because what Dexter understands about people—and how to deal with them—can significantly change your life.

Not only has he raised seven of us kids, but over the last twenty-five years he's helped raise up leaders all over the world who are strong, inside and out. These are leaders who love people like he does, who are financially free, and who are spiritually and morally equipped to deal with the challenges of the world we live in. These leaders raise up other leaders—and so it goes.

My hope is that this book will give you a working knowledge of how to understand and deal with people in a way that brings you great personal success. As my dad says, "Success is the progressive realization of a worthwhile dream." Success is much more than money. It has to do with relationships. Because without the richness of strong and joyful relationships, all the money in the world won't be enough to ease the pain.

I'd like to share with you a few excerpts from personal letters that have come to me about Dexter. Not long ago, I invited people who know him to share with me any stories or events that stood out in their minds as typical of Dexter. Even though I can only include a fraction of what came to me, I want to share a few. What you are about to read are the thoughts about a special kind of man.

Dex is not a philosopher, although you'll hear his philosophy as he shares his perspectives on people and life. He's not a psychologist, although his grasp of how people think—and how they succeed or fail based on that process— is amazing. He's not a preacher, although sometimes you'll find him passionately preaching everything from courage to free enterprise.

Dexter is just a man with a big heart and a big dream. He's a man who understands people. He understands the inner fire, that desperate desire to win that drives every dreamer. He knows how to add fuel to that flame—with love. In these letter fragments I hope to provide a lens through which you can get a little clearer picture of the man behind this book.

> It was 4 A.M. on a Saturday morning. Bruce and Dexter were sitting at a small square table playing checkers. On the checkerboard Dexter had 5 black pieces and Bruce had 2 red pieces. Bruce, after studying the situation, looked up at Dex and said, "I can't beat you—the odds are too great against me." Without a word, Dexter put his hand in the middle of the checkerboard and turned the board around. Now he had the 2 red pieces and Bruce had the 5 black pieces. With a twinkle in his eye and a slight grin he said, "Why don't we keep playing and see how it turns out?" The game continued, with the odds now reversed. After about ten minutes Dexter won. I saw clearly the lesson Dexter was teaching us: that successful people never, never quit—no matter what the odds appear to be.
>
> —Bob Candler

Without question, the number one skill that Dexter exhibits (and has attempted to teach me over the years) is an incredible belief in people. That's why Dex is who he is. It's the easiest way to identify him. His dream is so big, and it's there not only for himself, Birdie, and his kids, but for other people—like Nancy, me, and our kids. Dexter came into our lives at a time when I had very little belief in myself. I had a little bit of a dream and lots of energy, but no confidence that I could achieve anything. But Dexter's message to me from the very first was simply, "Don, you can do it." He breathed the breath of belief into me when the rest of the world was saying, "No, you can't; no, you can't; no, you can't." His belief in me was crucial to our success because it held me up until I had some belief of my own. As far as I'm concerned, it's the most important skill Dexter has. He's a believer in people.

—Don Wilson

When I came to the USA, I had a low self-esteem and a poor self-image. As a new Hispanic in this country, I thought there was no chance for me. I didn't know English, and because my family is poor, I thought I was going to be poor too. I was a Christian but did not believe in myself. I didn't believe I could be somebody. In 1989 I got involved in studying the books and tapes from the Yager educational system. Through use of a dictionary and a translator, I started learning Dexter's teachings about life, about positive mental attitude and success principles. It changed my life. In my heart I knew Dex really believed what he was saying. I felt he believed in me. I heard him say: "You can do it. It doesn't matter what your name is. It doesn't matter if you are tall and fat or short and skinny. It doesn't matter. You can do it."

He gave me hope, faith in myself. I started reading and listening more and more. In a function once, I told Dex my dream, and he looked into my eyes and said, "You can do it." Today we are succeeding by building a huge Latin American networking business. Thanks to you, Dex, we are going from Hispanic minority to the financially free minority. We love you.

—Jesus and Gloria Rivera

Dexter and Birdie have taught us so much. When they speak, a strength emanates from them that is quite phenomenal. Their love for all of us is most evident. They seem bigger than life and yet are truly humble... Dexter simplifies relationship-building skills so that the average person can understand, assimilate, and apply them to his or her daily life. In other words, Dexter teaches us how to be "real" by showing us how to have fun with and care about people, and also to be as strong and steady as a rock.

—Mike and Marjie Markowski

Dexter's personal concern for us always impressed us. He was interested in our financial situation and in the pressures that were on us. He didn't seem like a multimillionaire coming in just to give us some "talk." What also impressed us was that everything he said made sense. Common sense. He didn't say anything in lofty terms. He came down to the level where we were, felt where we were, and then dealt with us in ways we could understand.

—Don Storms

I've heard Dexter say that if others try to make you feel inadequate, try to make them feel adequate. Dex and Birdie's living example has proved to me that when people are of a mature and discerning mind, they will see our integrity, if we just keep on doing what we need to do while maintaining our respect for them.

—Tom and Caryn Avelsgaard

Dexter has an uncanny way of believing in someone until they begin to believe in themselves and what they can accomplish. I think that comes from his faith—faith in his Maker, in himself, and in other people. I don't know anybody who loves what he's doing and is more committed to it than

Dexter Yager. And he's developed the ability to pass that belief on to others. With that kind of faith and commitment to what they're doing, people can persist through the good times and the bad times without losing their grip. That's what Dexter gives to people.

—Bill Childers

One night I was saying bedtime prayers with our eight-year-old son, Ben. He was asking God to bless our family and our friends. Then he opened his eyes, looked up, and said, "Mom, I think we should ask a special blessing for Mr. Dexter." I asked him, "Why is that?" He said, "Dexter helps so many people that I'm sure he needs lots of prayers. I don't think he could do it by himself."

—Larry and Bobbi Hathaway

The Key to Success in Life

Most people don't realize it, but the most vital element of
success in life is the ability to get along well with other
people. You can graduate from a top university and get years
of experience in your field. You can become a technical
expert. You might even land a comparatively high-paying
job. But unless you've developed your skills with people,
you're not going to achieve very much in life.

Jack Welch, CEO of General Electric, said, "The only
way to gain a sustainable advantage in your endeavors
for success is by hard work and good, accurate judgment."
We all know what it means to work hard. But how do
you develop good judgment? You develop good judgment
by learning how to work with people successfully.

Here's the situation: Everybody's different. People
have different attitudes, different viewpoints, different
temperaments, different objectives. A lot of times our
differences can lead to conflict when we try to work
together. Conflict can show up in a lot of ways—tension,
fear, anger, lack of appreciation, rejection, and insecurity.

Actually, our differences—and the conflicts that come
with them—aren't bad. It's just the way the world is.
Conflict is everywhere. But how you handle conflict—
and especially how you handle people in the midst of
conflict—makes all the difference in the world. I can tell
you this: When you "go to war" with people over issues
without relating to them as persons, it always costs you a
lot more than you gain.

Conflicts aren't just between people. We've got conflicts
inside ourselves. We've all got needs and desires that compete with each other. We struggle with our own feelings
about our background, our inadequacies, our fears, our
missed opportunities, our past mistakes. We're proud. We're
selfish. We're generous. We're disappointed. We're grateful.

Somehow we've got to develop an understanding of
what goes on inside ourselves and other people. We need
to know how and why people get discouraged and, just as
important, how they get motivated and stay motivated to
accomplish great things. We need to know how people,
including ourselves, work.

Just beware of one thing. Don't ever try to develop
people skills so you can get your way with people. Instead,
develop people skills in order to help people and to grow
in your own life. That's when relationships prosper. In fact,
they'll be more fulfilling than you ever thought possible.
Whether it's business relationships, family, or friendships, it's
the same process. People skills involve wisdom—knowing
how to do and say the right thing at the right time.

As you become skilled in dealing with people, you'll
discover that getting along with people doesn't always
mean giving people what they want.

I remember once when Ron and I were out on the
lake finishing up a great boat ride. As we approached my

boathouse, we could see people standing on the dock looking at my home. I didn't recognize any of them, but I was pleasant with them and asked if I could help them.

They said they were just looking around. I realized they were not business acquaintances. In fact, they didn't know me at all. They were sightseers. Understanding what they were up to, I responded more firmly. "This is private property," I explained and then asked them to leave.

They were not cooperative. "We have a right to see this house if we want to," they replied. But I repeated my request without flinching, "You have no right to look at my private property. I'm asking you to leave right now."

The people stood silently a moment, then turned their backs and were gone. I didn't become angry with them. But I didn't back down on my request either.

Does that example sound like the opposite of people skills? It's not. Listen. There are times you'll deal with people who'll try to force you into a negative position—and even take advantage of you if they can. People skills involve not only building positive, loving relationships, but also being firm when you need to be firm.

Just after my wife, Birdie, and I moved to our new house in Charlotte, I stopped in at a hardware store to get some handles and hinges. When I checked out I told the clerk, "I'm Dexter Yager, and I'd like to charge these to Yager Construction Company."

The clerk was friendly and polite as he checked his records. Then he said, "I'm sorry, sir, you're not on the list of those who have charging privileges." I just smiled at him. "I own Yager Construction Company," I said, "and I think it will be fine." But he insisted, "No, sir, it's our policy. You're not on the list, and I can't break our policy."

So I said, "Young man, I understand your policy, and I want you to handle this in the best way. Please do whatever you need to do to work this out."

Eventually, the clerk called Yager Construction Company and was told, "Yes, that's Dexter Yager. He owns the company. Give him whatever he needs." The man came back and apologized. I said, "No problem," and took my hardware and drove on home.

It wouldn't have done any good to get mad at the clerk. He was doing what he'd been trained to do. We've got to understand when to be firm and when to be gentle with people. Wisdom lies in knowing the difference. And we need skills in both directions.

It's absolutely essential that we learn to get along well with other people. More opportunities are smashed on the rocks of disappointment because relationships fail than for any other reason. It's not failures in technical skill or knowledge that most often destroy projects. Most of the time it's a failure to get along with people—coworkers, supervisors, customers, employees.

That's why companies all over America and the world are pouring time and money into training their people in personal development—getting along well with other people. If this investment pays off for corporations, think how valuable it could be for each one of us individually.

That's what this book is all about—dynamic people skills. Ron and I want to give you practical information on getting along with others—information you can put to use in your own life. Of course, this isn't the final word on such a vast subject. But we believe if you can master the basics, you'll find yourself miles ahead. The principles and advice in this book have worked for us, and we guarantee they can work for you, too!

PART One

Developing Dynamic Relationships

Situations Change
When You Change

There are two views about personal change and responsibility:
We aren't responsible so we have the right to blame others for
our failures, or we are personally responsible for our thinking,
actions, and activities. The way we live our lives reveals which
view we hold.

> After one of my speaking engagements in Louisville,
> Kentucky, I noticed a man who had waited on the sidelines
> a long time to talk with me. As the crowd thinned out, he
> made his way over and asked me if I could take a moment
> to talk to him.

"What you said challenged me," he said sincerely. "And
I definitely need to make changes in my life. I know I
need it in my marriage, in my finances—and I try so hard.
But it seems like I get right to the edge of making a major
difference, and then I pull back. Am I scared? Am I *immature?*
What's my problem?"
  We spent the next ten or fifteen minutes talking about
what this man should do next. But I'll never forget that

question and the fervency in his face. "I get so close—and then I pull back. Is there any way to stop the frustration and create permanent change?"

Here's the good news: You can create permanent change in your life. There is a way to get beyond mediocrity and gain self-respect. But you can't play games anymore—not with your bank account, your personal dignity, your marriage— or anything else that matters. You can create positive changes in any area of your life. But here's the key: Situations change only when you change.

So how do you make lasting changes in your own individual experience? Here's the first step: You must be willing to grow up.

Growing Up

Childhood is great. And it's a good thing to be a kid— when you're a kid. But a lot of times people hang on to childish attitudes when it's time to grow up and become an adult. Most of the chronic problems I see in people's lives are there because they don't want to grow up and take responsibility for their situation. They want somebody else to fix it.

But nobody else is going to fix it. In fact, nobody else can. Growing up means taking responsibility instead of shrugging it off. The common thinking of our society today makes it easy for us to blame other people for our situations. "If it weren't for my boss... my teacher... my parents...." As someone once said, "We seem to have a general romance in America with being a victim."

It's a common thing today to hear people talking about their rights being violated. In fact, there's almost a "rights obsession" in our society today. Somewhere we got the idea that our rights are more important than anyone else's.

It's gotten to where people have begun to believe it's their personal right to have every selfish thing they want.

I read about an FBI agent who stole two thousand dollars, went to Atlantic City, and gambled it all away. But recently he was reinstated because he successfully argued in court that he had a "gambling handicap," so he couldn't help it. Therefore, he shouldn't be dismissed from his job. Amazing.

An employee of a school district was fired for being late too many times. She sued her employer because she said she's a victim of "chronic lateness syndrome," so being late was not her fault.

Obviously, if you're a victim of your circumstances, you can't change anything. Victims are victims. But the first key to changing things is to grow up! Step out of the "poor me I'm just a victim" mentality and take responsibility for where you are in life. Say, "Where I am is no one else's fault. I am responsible for my own actions, and I won't waste my time blaming others."

If you're going to be a success, you're going to have to be an adult to do it. And to be an adult, you've got to relate to other people as an adult. In order to grow in people skills, you've got to grow up first. Spanish novelist Fernando Diaz Plaja wrote, "Children who don't grow up become adults who cause problems."

So now you're probably wondering: "Am I grown up or am I not?" Good question. A lot of people assume they're grown up when actually they're still operating like teenagers. Teenagers, for example, are ego-centered. They're more concerned with their own feelings than anybody else's. They're vain. They're always concerned with how they look. They're stubborn. They want what they want and get disgruntled if they don't get it.

So get as honest as you can for a minute. Just between you and yourself, what do you see when you look in a mirror? Are you more concerned with your own feelings than with other with people's feelings? Do you tend to be preoccupied with how you look? Do you want your own way and get irritable if you don't get it? Then you've probably got some growing up to do.

Characteristics of an Immature Person

As a teenager, you had some immature characteristics that you're going to have to step out of if you're going to be a successful adult. So as long as you're taking an honest look at yourself, why don't you consider these pitfalls and see if any of them are still operating in your life?

1. LIVING IN THE IMMEDIATE. Teenagers make impulsive decisions in response to how they feel. They live in the "right here, right now" without regard to consequences down the road. Delayed gratification is tough because they want satisfaction immediately. They base their decisions on the desire of the moment.

2. SHORT ON DISCIPLINE. Teenagers want to be free to do what they want to do when they feel like doing it. But discipline is what brings us into adult maturity.

Discipline is the greatest battle some of us fight. One man, for instance, told me he'd prayed and prayed, asking God to help him get up early enough in the morning for him to study his Bible before work. But he continually overslept, so he wondered if God just didn't want him to read his Bible. That's an immature thought. The truth is he hadn't taken responsibility for fulfilling his own priorities.

All of us need more discipline. God isn't under any obligation to send a band of angels to get us out of bed in the morning. We've got to do it. That's true of any situation, whether it's in business or personal life. Teenagers look at discipline as a drag and a burden. Adults have discovered that it's the doorway to freedom. It frees you to succeed.

3. DOMINATED BY EMOTIONS. When your feelings control what you do, thinking is limited. For adolescents, everything is controlled by the emotions of the moment. If two people get married and both of them are still operating like teenagers, they're probably going to have furious fights because they're still dominated by their emotions.

Have you ever bought something you couldn't really afford just because you felt like it? If so, you were dominated by emotion. Thousands of dollars in ongoing credit card balances testify to the widespread adolescence of adults in America.

4. LIMITED KNOWLEDGE WITHOUT KNOWLEDGE OF THE LIMITS. Although teenagers are limited in their knowledge of life, sex, people, and experience, they're unaware of those limitations. They think of themselves as knowledgeable and experienced. The same can be true for anyone at any age who hasn't expanded their awareness of life. They may have extremely limited knowledge, yet they act like they know everything.

5. OPERATING FROM A SENTIMENTALITY BASE, NOT A REALITY BASE. Ron told me that during his first year of college he got a crush on a girl he'd only met one time. Since the girl lived four hundred miles away, it was easy to be sentimental. He created a great romance in his imagination. He even decided he would marry her. Finally, he drove to her home for a visit. When he got there, reality set in. For one thing, she was dating someone else. Things were not at all what he'd imagined them to be. He began to realize he couldn't possibly be thinking seriously about marriage. The truth was, he didn't even know the girl!

Imagining things to be the way they're not is sentimentality. You may have the sentimental idea that you can be three months late on your house payment and the bank will understand. But the truth is, you shouldn't be shocked when an attorney calls announcing foreclosure on your home. That's reality, not sentimentality.

6. SEXUALLY ABSORBED. Teenagers think about sex a lot—sometimes excessively. Although sexual desire is natural, it becomes more balanced as you grow into adulthood. Sadly, some men and women have brutally wrecked their marriages and destroyed the hearts of their children because they allowed sex to control them, rather than controlling it. For adults, the exercising of their sexuality supports their dreams. For teenagers, the exercising of their sexuality is their dream.

7. IDENTITY SENSITIVE. Adolescents are always deeply concerned about how they're coming across to other people. A person who gives up his or her business dreams because someone else doesn't approve or agree may be stuck in adolescence. An adult is independent and has strength. Adults can stand on their own two feet and pursue their dreams, even in the face of obstacles and serious opposition. But identity-sensitive teenagers are only secure when they conform, doing whatever their crowd is doing.

So where do you stand? Are you always concerned about how people are seeing you? If so, it's time to step out of your identity sensitivity and determine your own goals in life. As you do, a whole new set of challenges will confront you.

Ten Obstacles to Personal Change
So let's say you're willing to grow up. You're ready to quit seeing yourself as a victim of your circumstances. You're

ready for the discipline, the reality, and the independence of adult success. How do you break through, climb over, tunnel under, and crash through the barriers and become free to succeed in your own life?

Ron and I are convinced there are ten personal obstacles or battles you must face, fight, and win before you'll ever see the permanent, positive changes you want.

1. GET RID OF THE "POSITIVE COVER." Positive thinking, when it's genuine, is a powerful thing. But some people are actually negative thinkers who put up a positive camouflage, so other people don't notice it. Here's an example: A certain man was chosen to lead a new management team. His supervisors thought he was a positive thinker because he was always slapping people on the back and telling them, "Of course that can be done." But when it came right down to it, the man flopped as a leader. Even though his talk was always positive and supportive, he didn't follow through on the work side of the picture. So despite his positive public image, his results showed that he didn't really believe on the inside what he said on the outside.

As a football coach said to his players, "You keep talking about being the best, and you strut around saying you're number one. Well, now it's time for those of you who talk the talk to walk the walk."

How about you? Have you created a "positive cover" in certain areas of your life? You know how to talk the talk, but you've never really stuck your neck out and put your life on the line. It's easy to fool people who don't know you very well with a positive cover. But unless that cover comes off, you won't grow in people skills. Being authentic is the first lesson in relating to people, including yourself.

2. AVOID THE "HIDDEN HOOKS" OF LIFE. Sometimes we get into patterns of behavior that meet our needs

temporarily but do a lot of damage in the long run. For
example, maybe when you're under pressure, you scream at
your kids. Or whenever someone rubs you the wrong way,
you lash out with sarcasm. Or when somebody challenges
you, you back off. The more times you repeat a negative
pattern, the harder it is to break free of it. These patterns can
become "hooks" in our life.

Let's say a married man is having his sexual needs met
by another woman. In the process, he's breaking his vows
to his wife and violating his personal, moral, and spiritual
integrity. He struggles when he realizes that what he's
doing is wrong and that he really loves his wife. Yet he
keeps repeating the same wrongful pattern of response.
Sexual tension builds, he again turns to the other woman,
he repents, and then he goes back to his wife. When he
finally decides to end the adultery, he chooses the wrong
time to talk to the other woman—late at night in her
apartment—and sex becomes a hidden hook in his life
one more time. This man's pattern of getting his needs
met will destroy him—and his family—unless he can
break this pattern.

When a wrong pattern is meeting a need in your life, even
temporarily, it becomes a hook. And to get free you're going
to have to break the power of that hook. In the example I
just told you, the man should have written the other woman
a note to end it. He should have made the choice never to see
her again, to repent before God, and to return to his wife,
never allowing sexual sin to hook him again.

These hidden hooks in life create our addictions. When
you use something that's not healthy to meet a need, it
actually creates a greater need. At some point you have
to take a look at those patterns in your life and choose to

stop them. You can't go forward to success while you're still
going around in the circle that has gotten you nowhere.

3. LET GO OF YOUR "COMFORT BLANKET." A
"comfort blanket" is what you carry around—more mentally
than physically once you reach adulthood—that makes
you feel secure. For most people it's a certain measure of
mediocrity that makes them feel safe. They take a "middle of
the road" course in life that's neither hot nor cold, but safe
and cautious. But mediocrity is what happens automatically
once you make a decision not to stick your head out because
it might get shot off. So, instead, you begin to sink down into
the quicksand of being mediocre and obliterate the chance
for any real success.

During the Battle of Gettysburg, there were at least three
different occasions when General Lee's forces could have
won and ended the American Civil War in favor of the
Confederacy. But each time, there were officers that failed
to move at the critical moment because they didn't want to
risk career embarrassment. In "playing it safe," they literally
lost the war.

Ron consulted with a small business recently that had
lost its CEO due to a low salary. When he asked them
why they hadn't paid him more, they told him they were
struggling financially, so they'd decided to cut the CEO
salary in half. In trying to cut down their risk, they had
actually sown the seeds of failure and cut themselves off
from the possibility of wonderful success.

People do it all the time. They hang on to what they think
is security and safety—and finally disappear into the quicksand of mediocrity. If you're going to have any real success in
life, it's time to put your comfort blanket down and decide
to make the sacrifices and take the risks that are necessary to
create your dreams.

4. GIVE UP DECEPTIVE DESIRES. When you have a desire, either back it up with action or let it go. To believe you want something you're not doing anything to achieve is actually deceptive.

A junior executive walked up to a high-ranking officer who played the guitar and said, "I've always wanted to play the guitar. Can you give me some pointers?" "Sure," the officer said. "Let's start with what you already know. Give me a few chords." Embarrassed, the executive told him he didn't know any. "To be honest, I've never even picked up a guitar. I just always thought it would be fun to play one," he said.

When you desire something without the commitment to take action toward it, that desire is deceptive. It's empty. So check and see what you really want in life. Get honest. Flush out every desire that isn't worth the price to you. Once you know what you want, put action behind it, and you're on the road to success.

5. QUIT BEING SUSPICIOUS OF CHANGE. Sometimes people are afraid of change because they assume that anything different is automatically worse. But change is actually positive power. It accelerates and expands you into new areas of experience, excitement, enjoyment, and achievement. It's fun!

I know how easy it is, though, to get used to the status quo and start avoiding change. When we first started making changes in our home, changing rooms and furniture around, I didn't like it. I had become comfortable with things the way they were. But I made a decision to enjoy the change instead of fighting it. After a few days I really liked it better! Change is not your enemy. It's part of the healthy progress of life.

Change doesn't threaten people who are secure and stable at the core of their being. The Bible teaches that God is a God of orderliness—and orderliness is beneficial to our well-being and balance in life. So change is never chaos. Experts in mental health say that people who are psychologically healthy are people who enjoy the challenge and excitement of change. They don't resist it. They hop on board. They ride the wave and have a great ride. So get off the beach and come on in. The water's fine!

6. SPRING THE TRAP OF SMALL THINKING. It's easy to be trapped by the trivialities of everyday life. But whenever you let yourself be seduced into small thinking, you get so absorbed in it that you have no energy left for the higher levels of achievement.

How many times do we hear people tell us, "I just don't have time to do anything else"? But when you look at the results they're actually producing with their lives, it's not very impressive. They run around the same track every day trying to make enough to pay their bills and contribute very little to the lives of other people. What's happened? They're caught in the trap of small thinking. "Busyness" has filled their lives, but their lives were too narrow in the first place.

Whenever you surrender to the small, you can't stand tall. All those little things that get to you are like tiny pinpricks that eventually let the air out of your life. When you let trivial things matter—when you care about petty stuff more than important issues and relationships—you've been trapped by small thinking. So no matter what trivialities bug you, remember this: What's trivial won't count in the long run. Relationships will.

7. DON'T IGNORE THE PASSING OF TIME. Every year is a complete cycle in which we have a chance to begin again. We can reach out and do better than we've ever done before. But for a lot of people, year after year goes by, and all

their good intentions fall by the wayside. They tell themselves: "Hey, if I don't get it done this year, I'll get it done next year."

Successful people don't operate like that. They know that if you ignore the passage of time, life will float by you. They know that procrastination is like a narcotic, dulling the senses with "down the road" promises that never come true. So how do you guard against it? Joe E. Lewis said, "It's true that you only live once. But if you work it right, once is enough." You've only got one life here on earth to live. Make sure you make the best of it this year.

8. AVOID FANTASY-FILLED FAILURE. A lot of times, people who fail create fantasies to convince themselves they haven't really failed at all.

Recently Ron told me about reading Shelby Foote's detailed history of the Civil War. It included actual telegrams from the generals of both sides to their headquarters. Almost all said the same thing: "Wonderful victory." "Great success." However, two-thirds of the battles were actually miserable failures—and the number of casualties defies belief. Now that's filling yourself with fantasy while you fail!

Pat Riley, the well-known basketball coach and author, wrote: "If you fill yourself with unreality in life, you will not be prepared for the thunderbolts." How true that is. If you keep convincing yourself that everything is great, all the while ignoring the accumulating evidence otherwise, you're living in a fantasy world. And you'll be a sitting duck for the thunderbolt of life that hits you unexpectedly.

So take notice of the areas in your life where you aren't being successful. Get honest and take action in those areas before it's too late to turn them around.

9. DESTROY LETHAL LAZINESS BEFORE IT DESTROYS YOU. In the *Star Wars* trilogy, the Jedi master,

Yoda, tells young Luke Skywalker, "Don't surrender to the dark side." For us today, especially in America, the message is "Don't surrender to the soft side." We mustn't give in to lethal laziness, or we will paralyze the power of change in our lives.

A college basketball coach was so committed to finding winning players that he traveled five hundred miles a week, every week, just to scout for them. He became a winning coach because he was so committed to his team's excellence that no amount of personal effort was too much.

That's what success requires. If you want to become the best you can be, you can't give in to personal laziness. You can count on this: The soft way is the way of failure. Success never negotiates its price.

10. QUIT SABOTAGING YOURSELF BY FOCUSING ON YOURSELF. One primary reason people fail in relationships is they think too much about themselves. It's not that they're rude or selfish; they're just consumed with themselves in their own thinking. When you concentrate on yourself too much, you miss out on the joy in life.

I remember when I first got into business, I used to stutter so much it embarrassed me. I got self-conscious. And that made it worse. The more self-conscious I was, the more I stuttered. But when I started talking to people about things I knew would change their lives, I forgot about myself. I started dreaming with them. I joked with them. Together, we poked fun at me. And I started to love them. I really did.

I don't know when it was that I stopped stuttering. I just remember that one day I noticed it was gone. I hadn't stuttered in a long time. But I never noticed when it stopped because I wasn't thinking about me anymore. I was thinking about them.

A lot of people ask me what's the secret of my success. Focusing on others is the biggest part of it, I think. Loving other people takes your eyes off yourself.

Even in the larger arena, you can see this principle at work. Eugene Debs, the first socialist candidate for the U.S. presidency, was a wonderful man. He had compassion and personally cared about people and wanted to stop the abuses of capitalism. However, he was mistaken in his theory of government. He thought socialism would take care of people. But as that philosophy has filtered on down into our government, we've seen it create a nation of takers instead of a nation of givers. And when people are taking instead of giving, things begin to break down. It's no wonder that that form of government has never had any long-term success anywhere in the world.

No matter where you look, giving is the basis of all success. Focus on yourself, and over the long haul, you will fail in life. Focus on the needs of others, and you will meet with great success. That's exactly what happened to me.

A Responsible Maturity

It's time to get back to the way we used to be in America. I was sad to read the other day, "Almost everyone today seems to feel entitled to all sorts of successes, adventures, and joys right now without having to make any great sacrifices to get them."

I agree it seems that way. But it wasn't always so. During World War I and World War II, Europeans looked at Americans as somewhat naive, innocent in their outlook, and inexperienced in the more sophisticated things of life. But they also saw Americans as incredible believers in personal responsibility. Some Europeans wrote, "If the

Americans believe it can be done, they'll do it. They're excited and committed."

That's what helped America win those wars—that sense of personal responsibility and self-reliance. They saw what had to be done and realized it was up to them to do it. And when they won, they rejoiced in their accomplishment.

In 1950 David Riesman wrote a book called *The Lonely Crowd*. In it he talks about two kinds of people. The inner-directed person, he said, "has a trustworthy character and builds his life on the stability and security of his family. Usually he believes in the Judeo-Christian faith."

The outer-directed person is "dependent on the approval of others, especially experts. They are consumed by a quest for personal happiness, so that... anything becomes permissible if it makes me happy."

It's definitely time for us all to grow up, to climb over the wall of our overgrown adolescence and get back to the clarity of being personally responsible for our own lives. When we do, we will start seeing some real and lasting changes take place.

We won't be childish anymore.

We won't live in the immediate gratification mode. We'll lead disciplined lives that are not dominated by our emotions but directed by our dreams. We'll realize what we don't know and humbly accept instruction. We'll operate on the basis of reality instead of sentimentality. We'll work hard at balancing our desire for sex and fulfilling it only in the context of marriage. We'll look toward God for our identity, rather than longing for the attention of other human beings.

We won't have to put up barriers to change, because we will no longer live in fear.

We won't run around putting up positive covers for negative feelings. Hidden hooks will lose their power over us. We'll feel free to drop our comfort blankets and step out into uncharted territory. We won't be deceptive in our desires or suspicious of change. We won't overreact in trivial matters. Instead, we'll see long range. We'll be always aware of the passage of time and strive to make the best use of every hour available to us. We won't live in a world of fantasy, pretending success where there is none. Instead, we'll take the action to create it. We'll refuse to give in to lethal laziness and preoccupation with self.

We will grow by leaps and bounds personally, and our lives will be changed.

Did you ever see the comedy *Arthur,* starring Dudley Moore? Through the course of the movie, a thirty-year-old drunken playboy, a multimillionaire, finally finds his direction in life through two experiences: First, by falling in love with a woman who adores him and, second, through the death of his butler—his truest friend and the father he never had. After his butler's death, the irresponsible, reckless Arthur says humbly, "I think I'll grow up now."

Those words change his life. He goes on to marry the woman he loves and to become a decisive, worthwhile individual.

We will see a deepening in our relationships as our people skills grow. People will begin to value their relationship with us and to trust our reactions and opinions.

If you want to be truly successful in life, you have to begin to show maturity and responsibility in your thinking and in your doing. People will be drawn to you, and you'll feel happy about the positive role you're playing in other people's lives.

I like what Immanuel Kant, one of the great thinkers of modern history, wrote: "Man should not seek to be happy but rather to be deserving of happiness. Man holds no deed that entitles him to happiness. He is only granted a charter to become worthy of it."

That's true. But here's the clincher: When you make an extended and determined effort to become truly worthy of happiness, somehow you stumble over it along the way. So welcome your greatest adventure—the endless journey to become the very best you can be.

Positive Patterns for Success

Everybody wants to be successful, but it's so vital to be successful in the right way. Some people are "successful" where their bank accounts or their status is concerned. But if they're living their lives on principles that aren't honorable, they're not really successful.

When I talk about a successful person, I'm talking about someone who lives by his or her highest values and ethics. I'm talking about someone who's developed positive patterns in life. A successful person is always productive, not just with regard to business or financial matters, but in relationships with people and with God.

Nailing Down the Nonnegotiables
One thing successful people come to terms with early in life is the nonnegotiables. Unsuccessful people ignore them or, worse yet, try to find ways around them.

Take laws, for example. Laws are legal boundaries in our lives that protect us and keep our society going. Successful people understand that. They understand that nonnegotiables are important. Even though some nonnegotiables are imposed on us, the most important ones are those we select ourselves. We have the freedom to choose boundaries for our personal lives. These are self-imposed lines we won't cross. They're important principles we won't violate because we know these principles protect us and make it possible for us to enjoy the success we're seeking.

Personal Nonnegotiables

If you haven't established your personal nonnegotiables, it's time to take a look and make some decisions. Here are a few of my own to consider. They may give you some ideas so you can start a list of your own.

1. HEALTH. If I don't have my health, I can't live a long time and enjoy my family, and I can't work hard to do what I believe I need to do. If I'm stupid about my health, I'm going to pay a serious price.

Because in my early life I failed to protect my health, I had a stroke in my midforties. Through prayer, discipline, and God's help, I have made a remarkable recovery. But I had to struggle and battle to come back. I had high blood pressure, and I ignored it. I ate fatty meals late at night, I gained weight, and I ignored it. It's the biggest blunder I've made in my life, and now part of my body still doesn't work properly. I want to tell my friends to protect their health—it is no joke. So, maintaining good health is one of my nonnegotiables.

2. FAMILY AND FRIENDS. There are a lot of "successful" people out there who are painfully alone because family and friends were not a nonnegotiable. They allowed other things to chip away at the time and energy they should have conserved for those they loved. They allowed foolish choices and slippery principles to damage the kind of financial

security they should have provided for family. Family and friends should be treasured. Putting loved ones first and caring for them is a nonnegotiable.

3. MORALITY. I know that immorality will wreck my life, break my wife's heart, and damage my kids. They can overcome it with God's help, but why should I rob them of the security and stability of a good home because I failed to establish some boundaries in this area?

Every day, we have the opportunity to be immoral in our business lives, in our sex lives, in the things we hunger for, and in the way we set our priorities. It takes personal strength to establish moral nonnegotiables and stick to them. But a fulfilling life, free of the devastation caused by immorality, is worth the effort to live by a code of ethics and draw our own moral boundaries.

4. SPIRITUAL LIFE. When I travel in Europe or Australia, I'm gone for days—sometimes for weeks. But one thing I never neglect, even with such a demanding schedule, is my commitment to study the Bible and spend time in prayer. If I neglect my time with the Lord Jesus, I begin to weaken spiritually, and then everything else is in danger—my family, my morals. Even my health will begin to slip if I neglect the spiritual core of my life.

When I spend time studying my Bible, the inner sweet, quiet voice of God speaking to me gives me the direction and the peace I need. There's no human experience that can compare with the reality of God's presence through His Son, Jesus, as the Holy Spirit makes that real in your life. Please understand that I speak from a Christian viewpoint here—this is who I am and what my personal experience is. This is one of my nonnegotiables. If I'm too busy for God, I'm *too* busy.

Sticking to Your Nonnegotiables

The reason we need nonnegotiables is very simple. When we settle on a few major decisions in our lives, a lot of smaller decisions get made automatically. This saves us time and energy. For example, I have certain financial nonnegotiables. I won't buy certain things or get myself in certain financial situations. For instance, I don't talk to solicitors over the phone because I don't have the information in front of me. It saves me time and probably a lot of money.

When we violate our nonnegotiables, we always pay a price. One broken, lonely man poured his heart out to Ron. "I'm in bankruptcy. I've been drinking too much. My wife wants nothing to do with me anymore. My kids have lost all respect for me."

What had happened to him? Early in his life there were things that man never planned to compromise on—his time with his family, his loyalty to his wife, involvement in any other-than-honest business dealings. But over the years he began to compromise his convictions. And finally trouble came crashing in on him. Everything he treasured—wife, kids, home, money—was gone.

So determine what your nonnegotiables are and stick with them. One man I met said he never makes a major financial decision on the spot. He always sleeps on it first. If he goes in and finds a great car, he still won't buy it. Even if he has the money in his pocket, he always waits until the next day. I respect that.

Decide now that you want to be a moral person. Think in terms of making a "moral contract" with yourself. All your life you've made these moral contracts—like when you got married or when you decided not to lie or when you refused to cheat on your spouse, friend, or business partner.

It's a simple decision. But it takes strength to stand tall when the going gets tough. And it always gets tough. One thing you need to realize: People who live by principles, who stand by their moral contracts, are threats to the evil that's in the world.

When we refuse to compromise, we become targets to those who do compromise. That's another reason our relationship with God is so vital. We can find the strength there to stand by our decisions, our contracts. But if we ever decide to take the "path of least resistance" and let our principles waver, evil will eventually break through our boundaries and wipe us out. That's why it's so vital to know what our nonnegotiables are and stick to them. Without them, everything else we do and work for will count for nothing.

Developing Principles for Successful Living

We talked earlier about how nailing down our own lists of the nonnegotiables will make our life easier. Another thing we can do that will have a positive impact on our lives is to have a healthy, positive attitude toward life in general. We may not be able to control what happens to us each day, but we can control our attitude and how we react to situations.

Now this isn't always easy. Sometimes we let ourselves get too emotionally involved in the situation. Yet by controlling our attitude and our reactions each and every day, we directly impact our ability to enjoy life to the fullest. Each day. Every day.

Behavior builders

My own experience has taught me that a positive attitude goes hand in hand with living your life according to sound, healthy principles. Let me share with you nine "behavior

builders," as I call them, upon which I try to live my life.
They work for me. Perhaps they'll work for you too.

1. MAKE FRIENDS WITH THE REALITIES OF LIFE.
You know what? Life isn't always a piece of cake. We all face
both good and bad days. But there's an important principle
you need to understand: People reap what they sow. This
can be good and bad. It means the world in general reaps
what it sows, and all of us, whether we like it or not, reap
some of the good and the bad of other people's sowing. This
means that life is difficult sometimes, and the sooner we get
used to that reality, the better off we're going to be.

2. TAKE RESPONSIBILITY FOR YOUR ACTIONS—AND
YOUR REACTIONS. People are always looking for reasons to
explain why they react the way they do—their background,
their personality, or their temperament perhaps. There's always
something to use as an excuse. But the fact is, on any given
day, a lot of circumstances get thrown at us. And regardless of
the causes, ultimately we have to take responsibility for how
we respond to them.

Ron turned his ankle at a cookout one time. "At first
I just wanted sympathy," he recalls. "I was focusing on the
pain in my ankle, and it felt terrible. But once I made the
decision to ignore it and just go on, the pain receded. My
reaction made a real difference."

I'm not saying you can mentally control pain—or any
other circumstance—all the time. But our reactions do need
to become conscious choices as much as possible. It's better
to act than to react.

3. CHOOSE INSPIRING ROLE MODELS. When you
want to develop a certain attitude or react in a certain way,
think of a person who's like that already—someone you
admire. It could even be someone you've read about in
history who took a heroic stand or made a difference in

some way. Some people think of Napoleon as a symbol of courage or confidence, for example.

Abraham Lincoln could be an example of humility and vision. Winston Churchill, a picture of courage. Harry Truman, decisiveness. George Washington, honor. Rich DeVos, leadership. J. Paul Getty, a great understanding of money. Paul, the apostle, a white-hot passion for the Lord Jesus Christ. Billy Graham, integrity and a scandal-free life. These are people who represent attitudes and traits I admire. When I need inspiration in these areas, I think of these great people or others I know personally who embody them, and it strengthens me.

4. GET EXCITED BY THE POSSIBILITIES. A woman asked me if positive thinking was wrong for Christians. She'd heard something about the New Age movement being connected with positive thinking, so that made her wonder. But I reassured her. "No way! They got it from us! Why should we give it up? Positive thinking just means being bright, optimistic, and confident in life. And Christians have great reason to be that."

Franklin Delano Roosevelt developed such a positive personality, such a powerful ability to interact with people, that those who came to visit him would say they totally forgot about his wheelchair. Even as president of the United States, he was so dynamic that people worldwide saw him as a man of great strength and commitment and forgot about his disability.

Disabilities are not disabilities until you say they are. Possibilities are not possibilities until you say they are, either. Everything you can do or not do is in your mind. It's your decision.

5. GET A DIRECTION AND A MISSION. You've got to decide where you're going. Once you decide where you're

going, that direction will determine your decisions in life. If you haven't determined your direction, you start every decision back at square one. It makes life harder. Decide your direction, and life gets simpler.

Sometimes, you may set objectives, and for whatever reason, you might not meet them. It's disappointing, sure. But when you're driven by a determined direction, a few missed objectives won't get you off the path.

What does it mean to determine a direction? It has to do with the quality of life. Set your heart on a journey for debt-free living; for life that is God- and family-centered; for a home that is welcoming to others; for a character of wisdom and integrity.

Combine that sense of direction with a personal mission or dream, and you'll become unbeatable.

While you're heading in a positive direction, a mission will give you added energy and purpose. A dream, a goal, is something you want that you can pinpoint and describe, and you know when it's been accomplished. For example, maybe my mission is to send my son or daughter to a certain college. I need to set aside enough money to fulfill that mission. So I'm motivated to keep my direction of financial stability. Direction leads to mission, and mission puts that drive inside you to keep going till you get there!

6. PRACTICE FORGIVENESS. Everybody makes mistakes. And life is full of cuts and bruises and people who hurt you, whether accidentally or on purpose. Forgiveness keeps the path open between you and others. It also keeps your heart clear so you can love people. If you let pain or bitterness build up inside you, it'll cost you unbelievably. It's hard to be creative or productive when you're carrying all the anger and tension that come from the hurts of life.

Forgiveness is letting them go. Christianity says that when we forgive others, we're treating them like God has treated us. It means starting over, wiping the slate clean. God did this for us through Jesus, so we can come to a God who is a loving heavenly Father and not a condemning judge. Whenever I think about how great God's forgiveness is, it's easier for me to practice forgiveness with other people.

Here's the bottom line: If we hold a grudge every time someone wrongs us, then after a while we'll spend more energy carrying that grudge than we will getting on with our life.

7. MAINTAIN SENSIBLE SECURITY. Balancing risk with a certain amount of security is a skill you need to develop in your business and in your life. Adventure is great, but there needs to be a basic level of security for you and your family. Then again, "nothing ventured, nothing gained."

You need to take risks that will help you grow, but don't be foolish. Get information about what you're doing. Make use of the wisdom of people who have risked successfully and established a solid base of security. They know a lot more than you do. Take their advice. With their help, you can determine how much security you need and how much risk you're willing to take. Think it through in the light of your own personal mission in life, your own dream. What is it you're really after—and what is it worth?

8. BALANCE TIME WITH PEOPLE AND TIME ALONE. We need people in our lives. We need friends and not-so-close friends. We need business associates, people to play with, and people who share our spiritual beliefs and values. We need people who will help us and people we can help.

But different personalities need different amounts of people contact. Some of us need more time alone to get refreshed and refueled. Others get refreshed and refueled by having people around. It's important to figure out the type of person you are and to build in the time with people or the time alone that you need. If you're married, your husband or wife may not get refreshed and refueled the same way you do. This is something you two should talk about and then help each other make the right kind of "people plans."

9. LIVE IN OBEDIENCE TO GOD. I believe the most important relationship in life is our personal relationship to our Creator. If that relationship's not right, not much else is going to be right in the long run. But if our relationship with God is strong, His Holy Spirit is going to give us the power to live like He wants us to live and fulfill His purpose in the world.

So my last "behavior builder" is this: Live in obedience to God and in a close relationship with Him. Put yourself in a position to learn personally from the Lord Jesus how to live. Jesus said that God's two greatest commandments are to love God and to love others as we love ourselves. He said that living by these two principles can only result in good. So when we live as God wants us to live, we're following principles of behavior that will shape all the rest of our principles.

Productivity guidelines

We've talked about some vital principles for healthy behavior in relationships. But sometimes, even when you understand the big picture, you find yourself sabotaged by the small things. Here are a few guidelines on how to manage the little things that can take you down if you don't learn how to handle them.

1. KNOW AND CONTROL YOUR AGGRAVATION SCALE. Most people quit projects, not because of major problems, but

because they can't handle the small aggravations. A lot of marriages get weak, not because someone commits adultery or makes a disastrous financial decision or is violently abusive, but because of a hundred small aggravations—like where you squeeze the toothpaste or if you leave your clothes on the floor. Aggravations don't bother us as much when things are going great. It's when things aren't so great—like when finances are tight and emotions are stressed out—that tiny aggravations become hard to handle.

If you want to be a superperformer, you need to be aware of your aggravation scale. There are certain things that bug you more than other things. If you know what they are, you can stay on the alert and make sure you're in a position to handle them. You might be wanting to close a business deal and if you haven't charted your aggravation scale that day, you could find yourself unprepared for an irritation that someone might spark in you, sometimes unintentionally. It could disturb you and actually derail your business transaction or spoil the meeting. That's why you need to always be alert and maintain an internal control.

Aggravations aren't the big, colossal problems—they're the termites, the little things that eat at the base of the tree and eventually destroy the core of the plant. Be careful that little aggravations don't get to you. They can spoil your performance, distort your responses, and ruin your relationships.

2. BE WILLING TO STRETCH. You know how stretching works when you're exercising. If you don't stretch your muscles and warm up, you're asking for trouble. You could pull a muscle if it hasn't been properly prepared to work for you. That same principle applies in other areas of life too. You need to be constantly stretching in your abilities, your

disciplines, and your relationships so you'll be ready when it's time to really move out and accomplish something great.

In business you're either stretching and growing or you're stagnating and getting flabby. I found out a long time ago I have to constantly be kicking myself forward. I always try to sense when I need to be stretched. Sometimes it hurts, but I know I won't reach any higher until I stretch.

Even corporations are realizing this principle. General Electric, for example, started a program back in the eighties that helped executives get out of any ruts they were in. It was a "wilderness" type program where executives went out and camped and took on projects that were physically demanding. Most of them didn't even want to be involved in those projects at the beginning, but during the process, their thinking began to stretch and their confidence began to grow. When they returned to the corporate setting, they transferred their new attitude toward the corporate projects they were engaged in. They were stretched and empowered by an experience they originally thought they couldn't handle.

3. RIDE THE EMOTIONAL FLOW OF YOUR LIFE. Your emotions have natural movements. This is a part of being human. Learn to rest and relax with the ebb and rise with the flow. Sometimes you'll have to counteract this and work hard for a temporary goal, but most superperformers know themselves well enough that they know when to lay off. If you can identify your body's rhythm and become friends with it, you'll stop fighting with yourself and you'll make progress toward superperformance.

4. DECLARE WAR ON PERSONAL WEAKNESS. We all have personal weaknesses, and we need to be ruthless when it comes to them. But when I refer to weakness, I don't mean sensitivity, tenderness, and love. These are the

primary characteristics of the greatest people who have ever walked this earth, including Jesus Christ. Jesus was a man filled with power and strength. So by personal weakness I mean areas of personal irresponsibility or unnecessary fragility.

In 1989, *Fortune* magazine ran an article on General Electric's CEO, Jack Welch, which included his six rules of success. I like them. See what you think.

- Control your destiny or someone else will.
- Face reality as it is—not as it was, and not as you wish it were.
- Be candid, up-front, and totally honest with everyone.
- Don't "manage" people. Lead them by example.
- Change before you're forced to by some outside source. Be in control of the change and the pace of change. Be like the man who decides to eat a better, low-fat diet before he has a heart attack, rather than waiting until he has one.
- If you don't have a competitive advantage, don't compete. Either get a competitive advantage, or get out of the game.

These principles attack weakness and make us tough and durable, not only in the marketplace, but in other areas of our lives.

5. KEEP YOUR PROMISES. What's more precious than your word of honor? I remember Ron told me that years ago when he first started making motivational tapes, he didn't have delivery systems in place that would fulfill his "ready in a week" promises. In fact, it took four or five months to get tapes out to people. Some of them didn't react kindly to the delay. But he didn't blame them for

their angry reactions. He had defaulted on his promise—
and that's always a costly thing in any relationship.

You've heard this advice before: "Deliver more than you
promise." But listen to what's even more important: Never
do less than you promise. Protect your delivery system,
whatever it is. And if there is a breakdown, communicate
immediately.

Acknowledge the problem, apologize, and fix the situation.
Always keep your promises. It's vital to your success.

The Secret of a Superperformer

In this chapter we've discovered that there are nonnegotiables
in the formula for success. Each of us has to impose boundaries on our personal life for our own good and protection.
This week, how about starting your own list of
nonnegotiables?

We've also talked about principles of successful living
and productivity. But the basic secret is this: *It's up to you.*
You're where the buck stops. You're responsible for your
own choices, your own motivations, your own responses.
I just pray that you will do what will bless your life, your
family's life, and the lives of everyone around you.

CHAPTER 3

Moving Forward with People

You can move forward with people if you develop the people skills that not only create friendliness but also build lasting friendships. Just remember this—at the heart of people building is people loving.

So what does it actually take to build positive relationships with people? Remember that there's a vital difference between friendliness and friendship. A friendship is a deep bonding between two people. It's always a two-way street. You like each other, and you want time together. Friendliness, on the other hand, is something that's available in any relationship, whether you have a deep friendship or not. Both types of relationships are important when you're working with people.

Twenty-One Dynamic People Skills
In order to build friendships, you've got to start with friendliness. If you practice the basic skills I'm about to describe, you'll develop successful business relationships and build lasting friendships along the way.

1. PRACTICE A FRIENDLY FLEXIBILITY. More disputes are caused by egos than by issues. It's vital to learn how to flex instead of fight in most areas of life. Everything doesn't have to be your way all the time. In fact, when you're flexible, you're happier. If you've got certain rules that must be followed all the time, you're going to be continually irritated and disappointed with people.

I know some people who have homes that are like museums—picture perfect and untouchable. They look great. But you can't ever relax when you're there. You always feel like you're going to get something dirty or mess something up. A lot of people's lives are like that. They've arranged everything so perfectly that you can't interact with them without messing them up. I can tell you this: If you're like that, you're stressed out. You've got to be, because life never fits into a mold like that. Learn to relax. Lighten up. You can keep your goals in mind without worrying about the details. There are a lot of ways to get to a goal. If one route doesn't work, take another one. Set your goals in concrete and your plans in sand. It helps you get along with yourself and everybody else at the same time. Practice a friendly flexibility.

2. BROADCAST POSITIVE BODY LANGUAGE. The way you walk and talk is vital. How you sit, stand, smile, look at people—all of it makes a difference in how they respond to you. If you're relaxed and confident, they feel relaxed around you. If you're uptight and tense, they tend to respond the same way.

A recent study of business executives in America found that most top-level professionals will, in a conversation, relax and lean forward to listen to someone else. This communicates confidence and focus on what the other person is saying and puts them at ease.

How do you find out what your body language is saying to other people? Sometime during the day, when you're feeling particularly confident and successful, glance in a mirror or a window that will reflect an image, and just take a look at yourself. Don't try to change anything, just study yourself for a moment. That's how you look when you're confident. Do that a few times and you'll develop an awareness of that posture in yourself. Then practice the feeling that makes you look that way. People can't help responding to you better when you're broadcasting positive body signals.

On a long flight from California to Chicago, everybody on our plane was getting tired and irritable, including the parents of two small children. But as we got off the plane and watched those children—smiling, excited, full of energy—leap into their grandparents' arms, suddenly there was an amazing change in those of us who watched. We started smiling too. Our tiredness disappeared. The magical body signals of those children and their grandparents transformed the body language of the entire area where they were. That's what happens in relationships. When your body talk is warm, open, relaxed, and confident, people spontaneously respond to you.

I remember noticing a few years ago how President Ronald Reagan walked. He had kind of a western gait, his arms swinging back and forth—a very manly, friendly walk. John Wayne had the same type of walk. I was amazed at what happened when I experimented with that same confident walk—people actually moved out of my way as I came down the street. The body signal of that walk changed people's perceptions of me, and they automatically responded.

One word of caution here—it's important to be aware of how sexuality can affect our body language. You need to be sensitive to the fine line between warmth and openness—and what could be interpreted as sexual signals. People's reactions should clue you in to that. How do you know when it's OK to touch or not to touch? That depends on the situation and the people involved. But as long as your standards are high and others will not misinterpret you, you'll learn to recognize the boundaries other people have and respond to them appropriately.

3. KEEP YOUR VOICE PLEASANT. Nobody thinks they talk too loud. But the truth is, when we get excited or emotional about something, a lot of times we raise the pitch of our voice to drive home a point. This can really turn most people off. On the other hand, if you'll keep your voice level pleasant, it can soothe even potentially tense situations and make them work out.

I went shopping with a business associate last year, and in one of the stores someone was very rude to us. I knew my friend was angry, but I saw him deliberately lower his voice and speak very calmly and carefully. He said to the person, "This is totally unacceptable. We're not going to allow it, and you must change it." The moment he softened his voice, you could feel the tension in the room drop. The sound of his voice actually helped resolve the situation.

Voices are particularly important when you're talking to people on the telephone. If you want them to respond to you warmly, you need to work at developing a "smile" in your voice. People can hear a smile in your tone and the lightheartedness of your voice, and they respond to it whether they can see your face or not.

4. EXPRESS CONVICTIONS APPROPRIATELY. As a Christian, I have personal convictions that appeal to some people and don't appeal to others. Although I never abandon those convictions, I'm considerate in the

expression of them. For example, even though I deeply want my life to reflect God's love and I'm always glad to share with someone who wants to know how Jesus changed my life, I don't walk up to a store clerk and say, "Hi, I want to buy this. Do you know Jesus?"

Learn to be gentle with people. Never be abrupt, abrasive, or inappropriate. Convictions are part of who you are, but they'll quickly become obnoxious to people if you express them inappropriately. Over the years, I've watched many TV programs that involve people with whom I agree politically. But they were so brutal and nasty in the way they came across that I was turned off by their approach. Where is the politeness and courtesy in our country? Where is treating one another with respect, even if we violently disagree? If you want to have influence with people, treat them with consideration. They'll respect your opinion much more in light of your respect for them.

5. LISTEN ATTENTIVELY. Successful people are listeners. If you want to be successful, one of the first steps is to learn to genuinely listen to people and to ask them questions. If your main objective is to get your viewpoint across first, you'll never develop trust with other people. Research shows that people speak to the person's needs in a conversation only 3 percent of the time. That means 97 percent of the time we're more occupied with our own feelings than the feelings of the person we're talking to.

I was surprised to hear a man raving about me one time saying, "Dexter's the greatest conversationalist!" It's ironic, but the whole evening I was with that guy I'd been so tired that all I'd done was ask him questions—about his job, his family, his experiences. All I did was listen to him. But from his point of view, I was a great conversationalist. That shows how much people need to be listened to. If you want people to think highly of you, learn to listen to them.

It's not always easy. In fact, for some of us, listening is a matter of difficult discipline. I'm like that. I'm a natural talker. I get excited and plunge in. But I learned long ago to hold back and give the other person a chance to talk. He or she is going to listen to me a lot better if I listen first. There's a saying I like: "People don't care how much you know, until they know how much you care." That's a fact. And nothing expresses genuine caring as much as looking into a person's eyes and listening to his or her heart.

6. BE PREPARED. Sometimes you get a fear of people that's really rooted in a feeling of being unprepared for a situation. If you're nervous about what you know or don't know, your confidence is going to drop and your anxiety will take over.

Ron's told me about a recurring nightmare he's had: He's in a building and about to speak to thousands of people, but he can't find his way out of the building. He wants to go over his notes—which he hasn't done yet. He glances at his watch, thinking, "I can't find my notes, I can't find my way out, and I've got to speak in ten minutes!" When he finally finds his notes, he can't find his suit jacket. He runs from room to room thinking, "I'm going to be late and I'm not prepared!"

Most of us have had dreams like that. If you're not ready for a conversation and you feel like you're on shaky ground, it's going to be hard to get good communication going with someone else.

You've got to learn to read your own inner signals. If you've got that "I need to be more sure of the facts" anxiety, then go back and get the facts you need. Sometimes you need to back off, catch your breath, watch and listen for awhile. You may need further background information

about the person you're going to talk to. Preparation is part
of developing good relationships.

7. BE AUTHENTIC. People need to feel they can trust us,
that we'll be honest with them and have their best interests
in mind. We need to be fair and trustworthy and dependable,
always. All it takes is a couple of slips in this area, and people
will hear about it and start shrinking away. The Bible says that
God is pleased by pure hands and a clean heart. People like
those qualities too. If you're authentic with people, if you
genuinely care about what happens to them, they will see
that and respond to it.

Remember, you don't establish good relationships with
people by lying to them. You establish good relationships by
telling them the truth. However, you don't need to tell them
everything, of course. There are some personal areas of life
that people don't need to know about. But don't ever try to
deceive people. It will always backfire, even if it seems
beneficial at the moment.

8. FIND A CONNECTION. People are like islands—and
you're like a boat sailing around the coastline, trying to find
a harbor, a place to land, to make a connection. You may sail
around an individual for a while looking for that "docking"
point, the one place you can come in close and develop a
special communication.

A little girl named Gloria wanted to sell Girl Scout
cookies in her dad's office building in New York City. But
Mr. Johnson, the head of the company, was a gruff man
who had instituted a policy against permitting anyone to
sell anything in the building's beautiful marble foyer. Gloria
went to talk to him. In the process, she showed brilliant
people skills. In his office she noticed pictures of him doing
community service and getting awards for his projects.
Suddenly she said, "Mr. Johnson, I can see that you love

people so much and you do so many things for so many people. Because the Girl Scouts also help people, I thought you might let me sell my Girl Scout cookies in your foyer." You know what? Gloria sold her cookies in his foyer that year.

Find something good in another person and sail into their harbor at that point. Be like the little girl selling Girl Scout cookies. She zeroed in on a very good thing in that gruff man's life—and they connected.

9. BUILD BRIDGES. Wise people make it a point to build bridges to other people, regardless of how significant or insignificant they seem to be at the moment. Never, never make a needless enemy. There are great spiritual, ethical, and moral reasons behind this principle. The Bible itself says, "A man who has friends must himself be friendly, but there is a friend who sticks closer than a brother" (Proverbs 18:24, NKJV). This is the bridge approach. You need to be always building bridges to other people, regardless of the circumstances.

Even if you feel like someone is attacking you, and your natural tendency is to either retreat or strike back— stop and think before you react. What's it going to cost the relationship? If you retreat, you're building a barrier, and the relationship will die of neglect. If you fight back, you're generating hostility, and the relationship will burn up in the fire of that conflict.

So what is better? To practice the art and the discipline of bridge building—even when you're hurt. It's not an easy decision, but it's one that will pay off enormously. That doesn't mean you build deep friendships with everybody— that's not possible or even necessary. But no matter what the circumstances, you keep the lines of communication open with as many people as you can.

James Buchanan Brady, a New Yorker in the last century who was affectionately known as Diamond Jim, was amazingly successful. He was one of the first businessmen who used an expense account to develop relationships with his customers. He made a lot of friends and a lot of money, and everybody liked him. He had three rules for his personal success:

1. Win the trust of others by being trustworthy.
2. Win the respect of others by being respectful.
3. Win the friendship of others by being friendly.

I think it's important to realize there are times when you have to "love people at a distance." That means courtesy and respect, even when friendship and closeness are not possible. There are cases, even in our own extended families, when that kind of relationship becomes necessary. People who don't share our values or understand our goals obviously aren't going to become close friends. But we can keep the bridges intact by treating everyone with respect, showing interest, and avoiding disagreement as much as possible.

10. BE EMPATHETIC. Empathy is feeling with another person—putting yourself in his or her place and sharing their emotions. This can really help in resolving conflict within situations. Most of the time, people aren't purposely trying to be difficult. They just have certain conflicts they're dealing with, internally or externally, that you're not aware of. Another important thing to know: People aren't usually aware of their own prejudices, their assumptions, or their hot buttons. So be sympathetic and cautious. Try to walk in their shoes so you can understand why they do what they do and feel what they feel.

Learning to speak the other person's language is part of empathy. This isn't limited to other nationalities—the principle is true even when everybody's speaking your own

native language. Here's the question—and it's not always an
easy one to answer: Are you willing to cross over into
someone else's private world? Are you willing to understand
their mind-set and to communicate in terms they understand?
That's when barriers between people disappear—whenever
you're ready to step over them and love people in spite of
their differences.

11. STAND FIRM. Even when you care about other
people, you can't allow them to control your life.

Ron tells about a time when he worked for a church
in Atlanta. He had to go to a young man's home to tell him
that unless he learned to control his disruptive behavior, he
wasn't welcome at a special overnight retreat. The young man
reacted violently, accusing Ron of not being a Christian since
a Christian would love him and let him come. Ron assured
him that he did love and care about him, but if he couldn't
respect others, he still wasn't welcome to come. That young
man, even though he didn't come to the retreat, began to
modify his behavior toward others in the class. But his
positive changes started only after someone was willing to be
firm with him.

12. DEFUSE CONFLICT. Conflicts with people are an
inevitable part of life. You can't avoid them altogether, but
you can keep them short lived by using a few simple
techniques. First of all, when a hot moment arises, don't
feed the conflict. Defuse it. Stop talking. Don't defend
yourself. Listen. Get calm before you say anything.
Sometimes, you may need to go away for a few hours.
When you let the hot moment cool, it becomes
manageable again.

One thing I do when potential conflicts arise with
people is apologize. Most people are afraid to apologize for
anything at all. That's because they don't understand the

power of it. I'll apologize at the drop of a hat. I'll apologize for things that are my fault and things that are not my fault. I've found out that apologies are magical. They take the pressure of the situation off the other person and put it on me. That stops the conflict immediately.

The Bible says in Proverbs that a gentle answer turns away wrath. When someone speaks to you harshly, the argument escalates if you respond the same way. But a soft response takes the fire out of them. I remember a woman who left an angry voice-mail message for me. She was mad about some comments I'd made on a social issue. So when I called her back I said, "I appreciate so much what you've said. It was kind of you to communicate this so we could resolve it." Actually, her response wasn't kind—but the soft answer from me was gentle and effective.

The bottom line is this: Don't push people. When you push, they push back. When you attack, they either fight or retreat—neither of which will build a successful relationship. So practice a soft responsiveness with other people—no matter what their attitude is.

If something needs correcting in a relationship, make it right—*now.* Never procrastinate when it comes to healing a relationship. Respond quickly to perceived hurts and wounds. Undealt with misunderstandings will murder a relationship. The Bible says it this way: "Do not let the sun go down while you are still angry" (Ephesians 4:26). Don't give the devil an opportunity to cause havoc in a relationship because you weren't willing to respond quickly.

13. FOCUS ON A SOLUTION. When there's a problem in a relationship, your goal is to solve the problem, not win the war. Everybody has an ego—it's a normal human desire to want to be right in a given situation. But if you let that desire control you, you're going to confuse the issue and

contaminate the situation until no one can determine what the problem is, much less the solution.

Before you can solve any problem, you need to decide exactly what you want. That's common sense. But common sense is not so common as you'd think. Most people in a conflict situation haven't taken time to figure out what they want themselves, much less what the other person's objective is.

But you can't solve anything until you know what you're after. Objectives and solutions are going to fall into two categories—logistical and emotional. You've got to ask yourself, "What am I trying to accomplish logistically?" In other words, what circumstances do I need to change to make things work better? Separating conflicts into those two categories helps to clarify the possibilities in a situation.

In one of her books, Kare Anderson, a negotiation researcher and author, tells about a shopping center development company that was trying to buy a large tract of land. The wealthy landowner didn't want to sell it. After numerous frustrating attempts to purchase it at higher-than-market prices, the company called in a negotiator to help with the transaction. The negotiator first met with the executives of the development company to determine what it was they really wanted. Not surprisingly, it wasn't clear. Some of the executives felt they should buy the land immediately at any price. Others thought an adjacent piece of property would work just as well. After much discussion they finally decided that they wanted to buy the land. However, they were in no hurry and would sacrifice speed in favor of goodwill from the landowner and the community.

Next, the negotiator proceeded to play detective. Her objective was to explore enough of the life and history of the wealthy landowner to determine what his personal wants and needs might be. In the next few days she had informal conversations with nine local people. She learned that the landowner was in his late seventies, the retired owner of a toy company, and that he made regular and generous contributions to local charities.

Putting the bits and pieces of information together, the negotiator decided to try a different tack with the landowner. She wrote a letter apologizing for the company's repeated attempts to contact the landowner and asked for just one opportunity to meet face-to-face. If after that meeting, she promised, the landowner wasn't convinced that their shopping center would be of genuine value to the community, she would not attempt to contact him again.

The landowner agreed to meet with her. He turned out to be a sharp-minded man with many questions and suggestions as they discussed the different aspects of the proposed project. During the conversation, the negotiator discovered that the landowner was not considering any other buyer for the land. He simply was not accustomed to being hurried.

In light of this, the negotiator guided the development company in its communications with him over the next several months. She invited the landowner to the planning meetings so he could get a sense of the company and its intentions with the shopping center. Soon the landowner became an enthusiastic participant and gave substantial help with the child care and landscaping plans.

Three months later, the company asked permission to name the shopping center after him—if it became a reality. The landowner said he was honored but would have to think about it. Later that afternoon, he called and agreed to sell with only one stipulation—that his last name (not his full name) be used, so the center would be named for his whole family.

That's a pretty good picture of the way conflicts can be solved. First, decide what you want—both logistically and emotionally. Next, try to understand what the other person wants and how he operates. Finally, work toward a conclusion that satisfies the basic needs of everyone involved.

14. USE A "CAN YOU HELP ME?" APPROACH. If a wife feels that her husband doesn't listen to her, that he's angry with her, and that they're having conflicts in key areas, I suggest they sit down quietly at a time when they're both feeling relatively calm. She might say, "I know we're having problems in these areas, but I need your help." Most men will respond to that request because it breaks down the barriers and brings the other person into the solution process. It creates heart-to-heart contact between people so they can help one another find a mutually beneficial solution.

15. PRACTICE THE "DUCK RESPONSE." Just like water rolls off the oily back of a duck, let things roll off your back. Most people don't set out to insult or hurt us. Unfortunately all of us at times say things or use facial expressions that others could misinterpret as a hostile comment or expression. So it's better to give people the benefit of the doubt and assume that no harm was meant. Ninety-nine times out of a hundred, you'll be right—and the one you missed won't hurt you.

A medical doctor told me once that I have the lowest stress level of any patient he's ever treated. I believe the reason is simple. I just don't worry about things. If I can't resolve it, I give it to God and I trust Him with it. This is the duck response. You just let it roll off your back.

16. DEVELOP A SENSE OF HUMOR. Humor puts people at ease. It brings people's defenses down. Humor

about your own failings communicates to people that you don't take yourself too seriously, which is a trait of someone who is generally humble and easy to get along with. A good laugh makes us feel better physically. It actually works muscles that make us breathe more deeply. And humor can soften the blow when things aren't going well. After a point, you may as well laugh. It's better than getting angry or worrying about something you can't control.

17. EXPRESS GENUINE PRAISE AND APPRECIATION. Make it a practice to lavish praise on people. Not false, manipulative flattery, but genuine praise and appreciation. It's always possible to find something to compliment, even if the overall appearance of a person isn't appealing to you. Make it a point to find something good. Then observe it out loud. Praise is something people are deeply hungry for but very seldom get to taste. If you are willing to give it, people will begin to gravitate toward you. They'll find it difficult to leave you. And they'll look forward to being with you again.

But when you praise people, be specific. Observe what they did that was praiseworthy and applaud them for it. People desperately need praise for a job well done, but they tend to get embarrassed with generic, unjustified praise. It's much better, for example, to say, "Nancy, your work this month has been excellent," than to say, "You're a good person, Nancy."

Here's an interesting thing about sincere praise. *It reflects the values of the praiser.* If someone says to you, "What do you like about John?" and you say, "His commitment to his family"—it's immediately obvious that family is important to you. If you say, "He's a go-getter. He's a winner!" people can feel that genuine admiration coming out of you, and they begin to see you the same way. Here's the principle to remember: *Whatever you notice and observe in someone else reveals a similar quality in you.* Praise comes back and attaches itself, in the hearts of others, to your own life.

18. EXUDE HAPPINESS. People like doing business with people they like. If the employees in a certain store make you feel happy, you're going to want to shop there. It's only natural. So if you want to develop good relationships with people, become a happiness magnet.

How many times do you walk through a mall or an office building and see people with stern looks on their faces? No eyes meeting yours. No smiles. A look and a smile is an invitation to human contact, a disarming moment of friendliness. So be a happiness magnet. It's a great part of relationship building.

19. MAKE CHANGE EASY. We need to make change easy for other people, particularly if we're offering a new business opportunity, a new decision, or a commitment to a cause. Why? Because most people are afraid to change. But here's what they don't realize: *Change is actually an expansion of something that already exists inside them.* If they understand it that way, it's much easier. It's not an emotional threat. For example, if they've had a childhood dream of owning a Ferrari or a Corvette and you present a way to make that dream a reality, they can connect with it more easily. It's something that was already in them. Whatever change is involved seems "doable" if they're making it for their own reasons instead of yours.

20. BECOME A STORYTELLER. It's well known by the best communicators in the world that the most powerful way to get something across to somebody is through a story. Stories about people and events are more interesting to hear and easier to remember than dry instructions from one to ten. Stories also bring out more of people's

emotions, making the learning process livelier and more fun. Life isn't really about facts and figures; it's about people—their feelings, their actions, their decisions, and their results. When you hear a story about someone who did something and it didn't turn out, you can't help but remember it and try to avoid that person's mistakes. On the other hand, when you hear about something someone did that turned out great, you automatically log that information and use it to increase your own success. So learn the great art of telling stories. It works wonders.

21. PRAY WITH AND FOR PEOPLE. It's hard to stay angry with someone when you pray for them. As Birdie and I have developed our relationship with each other through Jesus Christ, our prayer life has been the bond that has made our marriage so strong.

Prayers don't need to be profound or complicated— they're just simple conversations with God. Yet prayer is a great way to release tension and reconnect with someone you love when times are difficult. Whether it's financial stress that's eating you up or you've been irritating each other without meaning to—or even when things are going great—praying together is a bond that makes everything better. God's love starts pouring in and solving problems inside and out. You can't really understand what I mean until you experience it. But I can promise you, it's worth · the time it takes. Stick with it every day for a month, and you'll see the difference for yourself.

Loving People

Obviously, there are more people skills than the twenty-one I've talked about here. But I hope you'll work on building these basics into your life, your relationships, and your work. You're sure to see positive, long-lasting results.

Above all, remember that at the heart of people building is people loving. Let God help you with that. Ask Him to give you His love for people, and you'll discover He's more than glad to share it with you. It always amazes me what a joyful, selfless giver He is—and what authentic givers we become as we let Him help us.

All you need is to be genuinely committed to learning how to love people. As you continually fine-tune your people skills, you'll build lasting and wonderful relationships—and this is what life is all about.

How to Stay Motivated Forever

If you're going to motivate others, you've got to stay motivated yourself. To do that, you need to understand what motivates people in the first place. And you need to understand what elements destroy motivation. The more aware you are of how motivation works, the easier it is to maintain your motivation—permanently.

What Motivates People?
Everyone is driven by the same basic needs. Not everybody thinks about them, but they are there. If you can't find healthy ways of meeting these needs, chances are you'll find unhealthy ways to meet them. But they can't be ignored. Somewhere along the line they're going to motivate you to do something.

Desire for respect
Everyone wants people to respect them. In fact, respect is the foundation for every healthy relationship. In trying to get respect, sometimes we go after success symbols. The kind of car we drive says something about us to other people.

The appearance of our house and yard says something too. Our personal appearance also affects people. Years ago I learned to "dress for success," and since then I've taught thousands to do the same—not because I have a dress code, but because I know what a difference a positive image makes. First impressions are crucial in developing new relationships.

However, we always need to be careful not to get off balance. As nice as it is to have those symbols of achievement and respectability, we need to remember that we aren't what we own. Material things are just things. They make a statement about us, so in that way they're significant, but they're not who we are. True and lasting respect can be gained only by being honest, trustworthy, and fair in all our relationships.

A sense of legacy
When we look back on our lives, we want to see achievement. We want to see improvement in the quality of other people's lives because we were there. We want to see our children and grandchildren in a good place and going in the right direction. How will you be remembered at home and in your community after your death? What kind of legacy will you leave? Ask yourself what you want to be remembered for and do it.

Need for financial security
Financially, you're one of two things: You're either a lease-holder or an owner. You may say you own your house or your car, but you don't really own them till every penny's been paid. Financial security is built on ownership. In the Old Testament, God's people were supposed to keep the property God specified for each of their tribes. In other

words, it was supposed to stay in the family. He wanted His people to have a secure place for themselves.

Desire for financial security keeps us working hard. Fear of losing our security is just as powerful. That doesn't make us materialists. It means we don't want the constant stress of being in debt and worrying about our children's future. By wanting financial security, we simply want to be owners instead of leaseholders. We want to own *things*—we don't want things to own *us*.

The Pursuit of Pleasure

We're all motivated by things that bring us pleasure. For example, one reason I work so hard is that I like to make enough money to buy things I enjoy. I also love to spend time with stimulating people. I get refueled when I work with thinkers, bouncing ideas back and forth. These are personal delights that motivate me. You have to find out what motivates you. It may be a certain kind of car or a vacation you want to take. It may be having time for friends or taking part in some community service. Whatever it is, if it gives you personal enjoyment, keep it out in front of you because it can be a strong motivator.

Unreached goals of childhood

Some dreams you dreamed when you were younger haven't come true yet. These unfulfilled dreams hold a lot of power, both positive and negative. I've known people who've ruined their families because they had a sexual fantasy as an adolescent and they never fulfilled it. As adults, they found themselves in a position of opportunity, seized it, and lost everything.

Childhood dreams are highly motivating. But it's important to look at them honestly, sort through them prayerfully, and determine which ones are worthy of pursuing. Some of them may need to be abandoned. But some of them should be updated and worked into present-day goals.

Desire for power
Sometimes, particularly when other needs are not being fulfilled, the need for power comes up. I remember once when I was counseling a couple, the husband said something controversial about a moral issue. I knew this man. I knew he didn't even believe what he had said. He was just stirring up controversy, trying to gain some momentary control. Obviously, this motivation isn't a good one. But we need to learn to recognize it in ourselves and others. It can be a monster to deal with, but unless we do deal with it, that motivation can swallow up other better motivations.

Desire for good health
Look at the mushrooming health-care industry in America. Last year the diet industry alone grossed over $32 billion. People are trying to be healthy. Testimonials of the power of juices to build your vitality now appear on late-night cable television. Vitamins and food supplements are finally being acknowledged as key factors in good nutrition. Wanting to stay healthy is a great motivator.

Desire to please God
Because I'm a Christian, when I talk about God, I mean the God of the Bible. The One who came to earth in the form of a baby, Jesus Christ, who loves us, died for us, and wants to dwell in us through His Holy Spirit. I know this isn't everyone's definition of God, but whatever your definition is, the desire to be in favor with God is a major motivator. It's a very productive one too. When you're

motivated by a desire to please God, you open up the possibility of positive growth in every area of your life.

Helping others

It's always fun to have nice things in life. Personally, I'm partial to speedboats, fast cars, and nice pieces of property. But the most powerful motivator for me isn't a new boat or a new car. What motivates me most deeply is helping other people succeed. I love to see other people get what they really want—and it turns me on to play a part in helping them get it.

Back when I was in high school, there were some big, tough, football players that were friends of mine. Even though they were heroes on the football field, when they went to a school dance, they turned into wallflowers. They didn't know how to dance. And they didn't want to take a chance on looking stupid, so they just sat around. I used to get a kick out of showing those guys a few dance steps—just enough to get their confidence going. I'd teach them the basics, and then I'd find out which girl they liked. I'd help them get together. It was great to see them win at something they wanted but would never have tried without some help.

Helping other people win gives you a thrill that nothing else can compare to. Once you get hooked on it, it surpasses almost every other motivator.

The joy of life itself

One businessman says his motivation is seeing life as an adventure. He loves the challenge, the excitement, the hunger, the adrenaline, and the sense of accomplishment. I'm sure that's what motivated the late Sam Walton—the sense of living life to the hilt, without restraint, and loving every minute of it.

Each of us is motivated by a combination of these factors. In order to be successful in using our people skills, we need to understand what motivates us and the people we work with.

Motivation Murderers

How does motivation die? What elements can kill it off? It's important to understand the fragile nature of human desire. It's powerful, but it can also be derailed by rejection or discouragement. It's in relationships with other people that motivation either grows—or is mortally wounded.

Withdrawal from relationships

When things aren't going right in our lives, sometimes we have a tendency to retreat from relationships and go into a solitary mode. That can be hazardous.

We have to be careful not to pull away from relationships that motivate us. Pulling away is easy to do when things aren't going right and you don't feel like you're winning. You want to hide out until things get better. But hiding out doesn't work. What's worse, it can kill off the very relationships that keep us going.

We're living in a time when a lot of folks are isolated emotionally. People move from house to house, city to city. Many don't even know their neighbors. Withdrawal from people is common these days. But it creates serious problems—loneliness, depression, even physical symptoms come up as a result of isolation.

People are important. You're not nearly as strong when you're on your own as you are when you've got people supporting you. You need people to help you stay on track and live by the principles you believe in. You need to surround yourself with positive, powerful, exciting people—and feast on their energy and enthusiasm.

Loss of energy

Sometimes you can track down a lack of motivation to physical sources. Maybe you just need to change the way you eat, or get more exercise, or maintain better sleeping habits. On the other hand, sometimes the loss of physical energy is due to another cause. Unacknowledged grief or anxiety could be eating up your emotional and physical resources. Sometimes it's good to check with your physician or counselor to pinpoint the reason for a decrease in physical energy.

Moral muck

Motivation is murdered when you get mired down by moral muck. I spoke to a man after one business meeting who told me, "I'm a Christian, but I'm embarrassed to say I'm struggling with an addiction to pornography that I got into years ago. Some of my friends are addicted, too, and we need a way to get free of this moral mess we've got ourselves in."

That's moral muck. It's a path of progressive deterioration. Once you begin to disobey God and break His moral laws, things get worse and worse. You start cheating, and it gets easier. You start lying, and it gets easier to do. The lies get bigger. I call it moral muck because it's mucky. Once you get into it, you just sink deeper and deeper.

Motivation toward anything positive can get lost in the mire of moral quicksand. Immoral choices leave a taint, a poison on the inside of you. They destroy your self-esteem, which also destroys your motivation. On the other hand, positive, moral choices build strength inside you. They heighten your sense of dignity and increase your motivational power.

Surrendering to doubt

All of us experience periods of doubt in our lives—it's normal. But you need to develop tactics for handling it, so when it hits you it won't knock the motivation out of you.

You've got to first put away the idea that there's not going to be conflict in your life, that if you're doing the right thing, everything will go well. It's not true. There are times when you're going to feel hurt, disappointed, angry, and depressed. Sometimes your dreams will seem impossible, unachievable. It's important to accept the fact that there will be days when doubt is nipping at your heels. *But make a decision ahead of time that you're not going to base any decisions on these negative feelings.*

When Harry Truman was just a struggling politician, he went through a time of terrible self-doubt. He knew deep inside he was going to do the right thing, but he had never expected "politics to be such a dirty business." Once he locked himself in his hotel room for two days. During that time he wrote a private letter: "I know that through politics I can help people... but I'm surrounded by such corruption that at times the depression sinks into me and the conflict tears into me; the headaches are terrible. But I know I'm doing right, even though it's tough."

That's a great example of admitting your negative feelings—and going on anyway. When you're pursuing your dream, the way is often tougher and longer than you thought. But don't give in to doubt. Don't surrender. When you know what you're doing is right, you can accept that emotional turmoil is just part of the price.

Friction creates heat. Heat comes from resistance. All change meets with resistance. It's a fact of life. And your efforts to build a dream will meet with the same thing. Heat. Discomfort. Resistance. It doesn't mean you're doing the wrong thing. All change can temporarily disorient you. *Just be careful not to let temporary disorientation produce terminal doubt.* Harry Truman would never have become president if he'd allowed the pressure of doubt to win. You've got to learn to work through it, to keep going, to pray, and to produce during these times. The state of confusion will pass, and your dream will be even more valuable when you know you didn't let go of it when the times got tough. Settle it once and for all that, with the help of God, you're going after the dream that's in your heart. Then keep going against all resistance until the job gets done.

Trying to be somebody else

When you're trying to live up to everybody else's expectations, you can lose yourself. And when you've lost your grip on who you are, your motivation fades. You get all caught up in the survival rut—working for other people's dreams and not your own. Your dreams are attached to who you are. So if you're going to maintain your motivation, it's important to stay away from people who cause you to doubt yourself.

Sometimes you can get sidetracked when you feel like you don't really deserve to be successful. If you're still trying to live up to images of what Mom and Dad wanted you to be, you may need to make a few adjustments. Only you can be responsible for becoming who you really are—for exercising your own gifts and talents and pursuing your own goals. Only you can decide what you want and what it will take to obtain it. Capitalize on your strengths. Learn to face your weaknesses and work on them. Don't try to be anybody else. God wants you to be you.

Gorillas from the past

These big, hairy, ugly gorillas in your life are the things that say you can never be what you dream you can be. They are the gremlins of your childhood, full grown. Maybe your gorilla is some damaging experience you've never managed to get past. Maybe it's a past failure or a person who always put you down and expected you to fail. There will always be people like that. Learn to avoid them. Get help in throwing off the hairy arms of these gorillas. Counselors can help us deal with old wounds and fears. Our faith in God can give us strength to throw off those monsters. And they must be thrown off because they are out to kill your motivation.

Laziness and pessimism

Most people waste time in the same ways every day. If you break even one or two of those small patterns, you can find fresh motivation waiting on the other side. Being stuck in our own laziness makes us feel that we'll never change anyway.

Sometimes, too, it's easier to indulge in doubt than to get off the couch. Laziness is always bolstered by pessimism. "It probably wouldn't work anyway. It'd be a waste of time to try." Pessimism is actually a form of emotional laziness, and it will wipe out motivation every time.

Guilt

Guilt comes in two varieties. One is legitimate. It's what happens when you do something you know isn't right. This kind of guilt is like the pain you feel when you stick your hand in a fire. The pain teaches you not to do that anymore. Legitimate guilt is a stab of pain when we do something destructive with our lives. It's God's way of telling us we're going in the wrong direction.

False guilt, though, is something altogether different. It comes in many forms—usually in vague accusations of personal inadequacy: "You could have done better than you did." False guilt also comes to us from people who are trying to manipulate us into feeling that everything is our responsibility. They punish us when things don't go the way *they* wanted them to go. But if we are certain of what God wants us to do—what is right for us—then we can confidently reject the guilt that others try to throw at us.

Staying Motivated

So how do you keep your motivation on track? I call this motivation maintenance. Here are a few simple keys.

Focus on your dream

Take a good look at yourself for a moment. Have you become content too easily? Are you satisfied with mediocrity instead of excellence? I read recently that "many people focus on secondary goals—goals they don't really want most." Perhaps you've done that yourself. Maybe you think those things will be easier to get or more acceptable to your friends. But focusing on secondary goals leaves you no energy for primary goals. Focus on a dream that delights you, that excites you—something you're willing to work for and sacrifice for. A dream is very personal. It has to be *yours*.

Remember who you influence

Constantly remind yourself of the role you play in the lives of other people. Ron told me that he asked his daughter, Allison, what she'd do if she got into trouble. She surprised him with her answer, "Why, Dad, I'd just come to you." Remembering how important he is in his daughter's life helps him stay on the right track.

Personally, I'm motivated by Birdie because I know she counts on me. I'm motivated by every person who reads my books and listens to me speak. Knowing the kind of influence I have, the kind of responsibility I have before God for the many people in my life, keeps me deeply motivated.

Remember honor and duty

Robert E. Lee said, "The most sublime and wonderful trait of character is duty." That's an old-fashioned notion in this generation, but it's a good thing. To do what's right, simply because it's right, without expectation of reward—that's honorable. And honor is a powerful motivator for a person of character. Of course, rewards motivate us too. There's nothing wrong with that, but we shouldn't be driven by rewards alone. Our world desperately needs people who are energized by a sense of honor and duty to their families, communities, and country.

Keep good role models in front of you

It's helpful to try to keep in step with someone who's going at a slightly faster pace than you are. Don't play it safe and always compare yourself to people who make you look good by comparison! Always be reaching out to match the better examples.

Get your daily surge

Don't let a day pass without positive reading and listening. As a Christian, I don't let a day go by without prayer and Bible study. When people say that God seems distant, I ask them if they spend time every day in prayer and in deep, intelligent study of the Bible.

Motivation won't seem real if you don't spend time in a motivational atmosphere. This is what one author calls "the essential power of a daily surge." When I get up in the morning I say, "Thank you, Lord, for today. This is the day the Lord has made! I will rejoice and be glad in it!" I say that every single morning. And then I get up and exercise, eat something, study and pray, and read some other positive material. I know that all day I'm going to need to ride a positive wave. So I need the essential power of a daily surge. And so do you.

Just do it!

Always remember the difference between a dream and a fantasy: One you're willing to work for; the other you're not.

When you don't follow through on your goals, you're carrying heavy suitcases loaded with fantasies. They require a lot of energy, but they don't benefit you. If your suitcase is jammed with unworked-for goals, it's no wonder you're going slower and slower in your life. Open up the case and throw out all the junk—whatever you're not really willing to work for is junk. Get rid of it.

Danny Cox, a former supersonic test pilot, wrote this: "In my study of achievers I have found that the difference between the great and the mediocre is one thing: The willingness to make a decision." If you think you've made a decision to build a great business and nothing is happening, *then you did not make a decision.* You indulged in a fantasy—because *action* is inherent in any real decision.

Open your suitcase and throw out the fantasies so you can have room for the dreams you are truly invested in. There's incredible joy in doing this. It's far better than the deflation of dignity that comes when you fail to make your dreams happen.

What are your true dreams and goals? To be financially independent? To have an incredible marriage? To develop a deeper relationship with God? You won't know any joy greater than putting all your heart and effort into making your deepest dreams become reality.

Danny Cox has another great quote: "When we were in the Air Force we had a saying: Some die by shrapnel. Some go down in flames. Most die inch by inch, playing little games."

Do you want to stay motivated forever? Then stop playing little games and reach out for your own true goals. God bless you!

PART Two

Knocking Out Negatives That
Spoil Your Relationships

CHAPTER 5

Deal with Regret

We've talked about some positive patterns of success, how to develop good relationships, and how to stay motivated. But just knowing positive patterns isn't enough. Before these positive patterns truly can become yours, you've got to rid yourself of any negative thinking that may be holding you back from establishing dynamic relationships.

One area of negative thinking people struggle with is regret. They carry their regret around like a weight upon their shoulders. But I can tell you from experience, you've got to cut your regret free and create something positive in your life if you're going to pursue your dreams and goals. Regret is a backward look. It means looking over your shoulder and focusing on your failures and disappointments. If you're going to be a winner, you've got to look forward with confidence in your strengths and successes.

Sources of Regret

Regret comes from two places. First, it comes from outside you, from external sources. Sometimes bad things happen through no fault of your own. They happen because of circumstances beyond your control or because of someone else's blunder or stupidity. A tree falls on your car during a terrible storm; someone else messes up, and you're left holding the pieces. So even though you didn't cause the situation yourself, you had a bad experience and you regret it.

There's another kind of regret that comes from inside. It's personal and self-induced. This is the hardest kind of all because you know what you did and the one you're mad at is yourself. You dwell on the "if only I hadn't done this" thoughts until the regret becomes the backdrop of your life. There are a lot of situations that breed regret in life, but I've found that most of the time it comes from acting on a selfish impulse, times when you stubbornly wanted something and you refused to negotiate with another person.

Let's look at some different sources of regret. Maybe you'll uncover some regrets of your own that have been holding you back.

1. EMOTIONAL BAGGAGE. Emotional moments— particularly with people you really love—stay with you forever. Even if it's something that happened years ago, you may still have vivid memories of painful incidents with your mom, your dad, or a good friend.

One fifty-year-old man told me about an experience he'd had when he was six years old. His aunt sent him a bow-and-arrow set for his birthday. He was excited and ran to show his father. "Dad, you're my best friend. Will you play this with me? You're the very first person I asked!" His father looked at him and said, "Son, I'm your father, not your friend. Go find a friend to play with."

Because of this painful early experience, this man found it difficult to relate to his own children. Specifics vary from person to person, but painful experiences are powerful sources of regret, and they don't go away by themselves. You have to face them again and make new decisions about them. If you don't consciously choose to react differently now than you or your parents originally did, you can stay hung up on childhood incidents forever.

2. HALFHEARTEDNESS. I've heard it said that Napoleon never had an introspective moment in his life. He was pure decision—a man of intense action and focus who seized opportunities. His entire life was a gamble for greatness. He did everything wholeheartedly—or he didn't do it at all.

One of the most serious regrets in life is halfheartedness in the pursuit of something you value. Halfheartedness is at the root of much failure in life—business, financial, personal, and professional. I don't believe Winston Churchill or Napoleon ever went to bed with a regret that they had been halfhearted. Why? Because they gave their all in everything they did. Halfheartedness will cause you much regret and failure. When you're doing all the "right" things—but you never give your business your whole heart, you're being halfhearted. Decide today to be wholehearted about anything you go after— whether in business or in relationships.

3. DELIBERATELY HURTING SOMEONE. A man was home during the Christmas holidays recuperating from a slipped disk in his lower back. He called out to his wife, but she didn't answer. She was moving through the house, getting ready for Christmas and chatting with relatives. So he called to her again. She still didn't answer. Finally he shouted out impatiently, *"I said something to you! Can't you hear me?"* She looked stricken; such behavior was not normal for her husband. Suddenly he realized that he'd deliberately hurt his wife, and a sick sense of regret filled his heart. He took her aside and immediately asked her forgiveness.

Often we hear of children whose dads deliberately hurt and embarrass them, whose moms deliberately ridicule them, whose brothers and sisters deliberately taunt them. Anyone who deliberately hurts others will experience a source of tremendous regret.

4. MISSED OPPORTUNITIES. Regret happens when we miss an important opportunity. Sometimes we simply aren't ready. Sometimes we are aware of an opportunity, but we freeze. We just let it slip by. Sometimes we're afraid of the changes it may bring in our life. But no matter why we miss these opportunities, they can be a source of great regret.

5. NOT TAKING CARE OF YOURSELF. One man said, "I have built a hundred-million-dollar estate—and I've ended up with a ten-dollar body. I've never taken care of myself." Taking care of your body includes eating healthy foods, taking food supplements, and getting exercise on a regular basis. No doubt you know that—but doing it consistently is another matter. Being lazy about personal health is a breeding ground for monumental regret in the future.

6. FINANCIAL MISSTEPS. Bad financial habits like undisciplined spending, careless miscalculations, and unplanned financial transactions can lead to regret that can plague you the rest of your life. It's amazing how people can bungle their finances—or simply assume the future will work out somehow—and never realize the terrible trap they're laying for themselves. It's important to connect with people who have wisdom in the financial arena and to listen to their advice. Find somebody whose lifestyle you admire, and let them guide you into financial sanity. Work hard to eliminate the regrets from the financial missteps of your past so you can step confidently into the future.

7. RELATIONSHIP BLUNDERS. Relationships are like plants. They need to be nurtured, cared for, fed, cultivated,

watered. Growth takes time. And unless you spend time with family and friends, these important relationships weaken. If you neglect a marriage partner—even for what may seem like legitimate reasons, like job pressures or emergencies—you pay an enormous price.

It's vital to take time to cultivate your relationships so you don't have to pay the price of regret. And if you've damaged a relationship in the past, consider making a sincere apology. Most relationships are not beyond repair, but regret won't repair them. Only humility and honesty will do that.

8. UNFULFILLED PERSONAL EXPECTATIONS. Unfulfilled expectations usually come from a perfectionistic view of life. But life is life. It comes like it comes. Life doesn't check to see if you approve of it before it hands you what it hands you. What determines if you're a winner in life is not the circumstances but the way you handle them. In order to overcome regret, you have to let go of unfulfilled personal expectations and determine to be victorious in whatever situation life hands you.

Why It's Hard to Deal with Regret

No matter what regrets you've got—a broken marriage, the failure of a business, or a disrupted friendship—you have to come to terms with it so you can move on. That's easy to say—and much harder to do. Regrets aren't always easy to let go of, because underneath our regrets is fear.

1. FEAR OF PERSONAL GUILT. Sometimes you're afraid that if you really face your regrets, the process will confirm your greatest fear—that you're the one at fault. You can't stand that sickening sense of personal failure. You don't want to deal with it. You'd rather sweep it under the rug. Yet regret still has the power to pull you down and drain you.

No one wants to be confirmed as dumb or defective, and that fear sometimes paralyzes you inside. It even keeps you from being honest with yourself and getting help. Don't let this fear hold you captive in your regret.

2. FEAR OF ONGOING DAMAGE. When you fear ongoing damage, you're never free of regret. You're in bondage to it; you keep trying to fix it until you're worn out. But the truth is, you can't live your life in fear of what may happen in the future because of a past event. If you do, you'll be a slave to the past for the rest of your life.

3. FEAR OF EMOTIONAL EXHAUSTION. Regret can wipe you out. Sometimes it's so tiring to try to get rid of the garbage, the negative events and feelings, that you're tempted to choose not to deal with them. But the cycle of emotional depletion is endless unless you choose to take the steps you need to get free.

4. POWERLESS DEPRESSION. When bad things happen and you continually relive them in your mind, you develop a past focus instead of a present or future focus. It's easy to focus on past events, but when you do, depression sets in. You wind up with a sense of powerlessness over your circumstances— because past circumstances are, in fact, unchangeable. So regret is a past focus—and past focus breeds powerlessness and depression. When you let go of regret, you can look ahead and understand that the future is in your hands.

5. SPONTANEOUS ANGER. Whenever you remember that moment, that experience, or that disappointment, your anger rises automatically. But when you don't deal with disappointment and anger, all they do is keep coming up again. Until you choose to get anger out of your system, it will remain there—trapped. If you're going to be healthy and productive, you need to take steps to get rid of angry disappointment.

How to Handle Regret

You may have wondered already why you accomplish so little year after year; why you can't seem to achieve much success. You don't understand what's holding you back. Chances are, you've got buried regrets that are affecting your self-esteem, your sense of who you are, and until you get rid of those regrets, you're not free to be a leader in business or anywhere else.

Successful people don't spend their time on negatives and regrets. They're forward-moving people, constantly creating the future and letting go of the past. How do they do it? They practice these nine habits for maintaining positive mental and emotional health.

1. MAKE A CLEAN SWEEP. Ron tells about a week Amy and he went through a major reorganization of their physical household. They even attacked a national disaster area—their closets. They had made a decision to get organized, and they got absolutely ruthless about it. They threw out stuff and gave away stuff—over fifty-seven bags of it!

In the same way, you need to make a clean sweep of the negative junk in your life that's draining your energy. Until you do, things will never change. If you're going to be free to become who you really want to be, you're going to have to force yourself to get rid of your junk. God will help you if you ask Him.

2. COMMIT TO A FORWARD FOCUS. I always have in my mind ten major goals I want to accomplish in the next ten years. When I achieve a goal, I replace it with another one. This process keeps me looking toward the future, so I don't have any time to wallow in the past. If you're going to be a winner, you've got to get a forward focus. Life isn't in the past—it's in the future. Forward, march!

3. BE YOUR OWN BEST FRIEND. Learn to like yourself again. Stop reminding yourself of your failures, and start encouraging yourself. The truth is, you'll be your own best friend if you learn to accept yourself and encourage yourself on a regular basis. Have you heard of positive self-talk? Learn to use it, and you'll go a long way in your personal growth and in your people skills.

4. DEVELOP A DISCIPLINED MEMORY. You have to come to the point where you refuse to remember negatives and failures. You need to discipline your memory. When negative thoughts arise and you begin to focus on your failures, ask God to help you think of something positive you've done instead. With God's assistance you can develop the discipline of memory control and free your thoughts for positive future ventures.

5. PRACTICE THANKFULNESS. Practicing thankfulness for all the good things in your life will keep you from dwelling on the aggravations that are a normal part of life. A few years ago, I had a serious stroke. I was in a lot of pain and experiencing incredible amounts of frustration, but I continually made the best of the situation. I remember parking in the handicapped spots in the parking lot. I could have been feeling sorry for myself, but instead I thought, "Isn't it great to be able to park in the most convenient spaces in the parking lot!" It was a little thing, but it helped me to stay positive in the situation. It's vital to learn and practice thankfulness for every positive thing so that the aggravations and frustrations of life don't wear you out.

6. GET A STRONG DOSE OF "SO WHAT?" "They didn't have my hotel room ready"—so what? "My check didn't come on time"—so what? "Somebody was rude to me"—so what? Unless you've got a strong dose of "so what," you can become a petty, small-minded person. I believe you can

measure the dimensions of a person's character by what it takes to aggravate him. Do little irritations wipe you out? If so, you need to give yourself a strong dose of "so what." When you have a big dream, you don't have time to get bent out of shape over the small stuff.

7. CONCENTRATE ON GIVING. If you want to over-come regret and be positive instead of negative, it is crucial to concentrate on giving. Learn to give, and make that the pivotal experience in your life. A lot of disappointments in life are due to our own selfish expectations not being met. Some of us haven't quite grown out of the adolescent, pouting-when-we-don't-get-what-we-want stage.

There's a great book out called *Iron Joe Bob* by Joe B. Briggs. In this book, the author responds to the whining we sometimes do about the difficulties in our lives by saying, "You know what? If you're going to have a dream, you're going to have to work hard. If you're going to make money, you're going to have to earn it. There are some times when you're going to get sick of life. There are some days you're going to be mad at everything, and you'll have to go out and succeed anyway. One day you're going to get sick and die. Well, face it, grow up, and get on with your dream."

One of the great challenges we face in America is that we've become soft and weak instead of strong and courageous. We've started moaning and groaning that our sensitive needs aren't being met instead of getting into the fight for achievement. If we continue this kind of passive introspection, we won't continue to be the world leaders we've been for over two hundred years. Why? Because it takes guts and determination to make dreams happen.

8. ACKNOWLEDGE A SPIRITUAL BASE. I don't know what your spiritual perspective is. Whatever it is, I respect it as very personally your own. In my life, I've come to know

Jesus as my personal Savior, so that's my perspective. But I've noticed over the years that the most peaceful, productive, and powerful people in the world have a godly, biblically centered base; that base creates the security on which they build their lives and their success.

9. BELIEVE IN YOURSELF. No matter how many times you may have failed, no matter how many times you've thought you'd do better, only to blow it again, do this one final thing: Commit yourself to believing that winning—in whatever area it is—is still possible for you. You can't ever do anything to alter what's already happened. But your attitude and belief in yourself can impact your success in the future.

History is full of men and women who won because they wouldn't quit believing they were going to win, who succeeded because they knew they were going to succeed. Although these people had experienced failure piled on top of failure, they ultimately won because they insisted on believing that winning was still possible for them, and they wouldn't quit going after it.

Turning Your Life Around

One of the highest-paid positions in corporate America is known as a "troubleshooter CEO." This person is brought in from outside a company to correct problems and get the company running right again. Usually he's brought in when things are desperate. He comes in like a lone cowboy riding in with six-shooters strapped on and takes over. If he succeeds in turning the troubled company around, he's a hero. He gets money and stock options. But there's only a handful of people who have been successful at doing this. One of the most famous in recent history is Lee Iacocca, who turned around the Chrysler Corporation in the 1970s.

If you look at your own life, there may be some areas in which you feel desperate. Things aren't running right, and you know it. As president of your company, you're saying, "Hey, we've got some trouble here. Cash flow isn't good enough. Our debt is too high. Our personal relationships need help right now."

Here's a challenge: Step outside yourself and look at things as if you were a troubleshooter CEO who'd been hired to turn around your own company. You've been given all the resources, support, and money to do your job. You've got permission to make a clean sweep and do anything you want to do, change anything you want to change. What will you do? Remember, you've been hired to produce success, to turn your company around so that by this time next year it'll be blazingly successful. So what exactly are you going to do?

That's a good picture of where you really are in life. You're the chairman of the board, president, CEO of your own life. The old is done. Forget the regrets. You now have the opportunity to start moving your life into a more positive future. You have a hero inside you. You really do. If you'll listen to that hero, you don't need to duplicate the negatives and failures of the past. You can institute the changes you've been waiting for. And come next year, you can say, "We did it! The bank account turned around. The relationships turned around. The marriage turned around. The spiritual life turned around. All this, because I took charge. I cut the negatives. I moved into the future with a positive belief in myself, and I did the job."

You are now sitting in the driver's seat of your life. What you do with it from here is up to you.

CHAPTER 6

Overcome Rejection

Rejection need not control your life if you understand why people act negatively and how that rejection—and your response to it—affects you.

When you were a child, you may have read *The Little Engine That Could.* In the story, the little steam engine winds its way up the side of a mountain, saying to itself all the way, "I think I can, I think I can, I think I can." After a long struggle, finally it breaks through to the top of the mountain and achieves the goal it believed it could.

As we talk about rejection, keep that picture in mind. As you go after your dream, you'll feel a lot like that little engine climbing up the mountain. Sometimes the way is steep, and the pressure against you is intense. But you *can* do it. You *can* overcome the negatives and work successfully with people. You *can* keep the steam in your dream.

How do you do it?

One of the first things you have to learn to deal with is rejection. But if you're going to win at anything, you've got to learn to take rejection and overcome it. There'll be times when people attack you verbally, emotionally, and you'll have to dig in your heels and say, *"No.* I won't quit. I won't give up."

Every leader who wants to pioneer anything great is slapped with the sting of rejection. I sat next to a woman on a plane a few months ago who had read one of my books and was initially quite complimentary. But then she said, "I just can't believe you would speak for *those* people." I said to her, "Ma'am, those people are the greatest people in the world. *Those people* are people who want to be free financially, to pay their debts with honesty, who believe in free enterprise and conservative values. I'm proud to be one of them."

I recognize there are some of you who still face this kind of rejection, this kind of misunderstanding. If you do, you're going to have to handle it properly and successfully if you're ever going to be the winner you want to be.

Rejection is a common occurrence in life. It happens in love, in friendship, in business. It hurts. Sometimes it hurts a lot. But if you understand where it comes from, it gets easier to cope with.

Why do people reject you? Let's take a look.

Seven Reasons People Reject You

1. YOU'VE BECOME A THREAT TO THEIR LACK OF PERFORMANCE. A winner mentality threatens other people whose approach to life is different. If they're basically lazy or unwilling to take a risk, your positive attitude will annoy them. They'll say to you, "Wait a minute. You don't understand. I can't do this because..." and they'll make their list: no time, no money, no education, no ability, no favorable circumstances. When you maintain your relentless "can-do" position, is it any wonder they get irritated and start pumping negatives your way? You represent a threat to their lack of performance.

2. JEALOUSY. Rejection sometimes stems from jealousy. Nicholas Von Hoffmann, who writes about today's business climate, has this to say:

> We have a serious problem in society. We cannot increase the standard of living for everyone without generating more wealth. And at the same time we hate whoever generates the wealth.

It's true. Jealousy is a real problem in America. In the Bible, jealousy and envy are addressed as serious sins. They are cancers of the human spirit. They rob us of peace, love, and good relationships. They create division, hostility, and conflict.

A friend of mine has an eight-year-old Mercedes that he's taken good care of. But when his wife parked it in a shopping center lot, someone took a key and gouged the side. That typifies the attitude we see so much today. Jealousy. Resentment toward anyone who has achieved something worthwhile.

Should we blame the rich? Business owners are the very ones who create jobs and build whole industries, who put their heart and soul, blood and sweat into a company to produce something that can help thousands of people. My response to this whole national hostility toward the wealthy and successful is "T.I.N."—"This Is Nuts."

3. RELUCTANCE TO CHANGE. I've heard it said, "Some people prefer the certainty of misery to the uncertainty of change." For some people, change itself is an enemy. When you come along and challenge them to take a definite step toward changing their situation, you put them in a position where they have to make a choice. That's the one thing they don't want to do, so they come at you with resistance or rejection in order to avoid the confrontation of change.

4. MISCONCEPTIONS. People don't know what they don't know. They reject what they don't understand. Sometimes this is the only reason why a person rejects you. So many people don't take the time to understand the dynamics or the principles involved in what we represent.

Someone told me recently that his pastor was against his involvement in a networking business. I asked if his pastor had ever been to one of our business meetings. No, he hadn't. I asked if he had ever listened to any tapes or read any of the books. No. So, I asked him, how can your pastor make an intelligent appraisal of what you're doing without accurate information? Obviously, he couldn't. His rejection was based on ignorance and misconceptions.

This happens all the time. Instead of doing their own research, people prefer to make judgments based on fragments of hearsay. These unresearched judgments are a form of laziness that results in undeserved criticism and rejection of things they don't understand.

5. MISTRUST. Sometimes people don't trust you. It could be your reputation. If so, you need to be totally honest with yourself about it. Do you have a reputation for poor decision making, mistakes, manipulation, or dishonesty?

If you do, there's only one solution. Build a new reputation. Work with respected people as your mentors and prove yourself in a new arena. Then, with your credibility reestablished, come back and talk to the individual who rejected you and work at winning his or her support.

6. DISLIKE. If people don't like you, they don't *want* to believe you. That's why first impressions are so important. I read in a marketing book:

> If you want to make a big impression on another person, you cannot worm your way into their mind and then slowly build

up a favorable opinion over a period of time. The mind doesn't work that way. You have to blast your way positively into their mind. Once they perceive you one way, that's usually it. They file you away as a certain kind of person and it's hard to become a different person in their mind.

So be careful what kind of image you project to people. If you don't know whether you're naturally abrasive or not, ask a friend, your children, or your spouse.

Try to build an image people will like. This doesn't mean that you compromise your beliefs and become a wimp but that you develop likability. Remember, if people like you, they *want* to believe you. But if they don't, they won't.

7. EXPERIENCES OF PERSONAL REJECTION AND DISAPPOINTMENT. Some people reject you because they've been deeply rejected themselves. You need to be sensitive to this. There are individuals who have had so much pain and disappointment that they fear their dreams can never come true. This creates in them a defensive response that feels like rejection from your side of the fence. But a lot of times it's nothing but the fear of believing and risking the pain.

People are afraid of disappointment. You have to realize that. It takes a lot of tenderness and relentless believing on your part to help them over that hump. But they can do it. If you'll keep believing in them and in their dreams until they can start to believe with you, great things can happen. I've seen it over and over again.

How Rejection Affects You

What do you think and feel when you face rejection? Some of us get mad. Some of us withdraw. You've got to understand what happens inside yourself to make the adjustments you need to keep going. If you don't, you'll let rejection steal your dreams and abort the future God has in store for you.

Here are some ways rejection may affect you.

1. IT CAUSES YOU TO DOUBT YOUR JUDGMENT. When someone says to you, "Are you sure you really ought to do this?" what you may hear on the inside is "Are you an idiot or what?" Something inside you freezes up because the rejection casts a doubt on your own judgment, and suddenly you're not sure if you're doing the right thing or not. I believe the reason some of you drop to the ground in exhaustion and choose not to fight back is that it's tough for you to have your judgment challenged.

But there's never been a successful leader anywhere that didn't have his judgment challenged. One of the true marks of leadership is the willingness to make a decision and then *make it right,* no matter what it takes. *Most "right" decisions are actually a matter of follow-through. Many decisions appear to have been wrong simply because they were aborted before they could turn out right.*

2. IT CHALLENGES RELATIONSHIPS YOU THOUGHT WERE SECURE. It's a jarring experience when someone you trust rejects something that's precious to you. Ron told me how shocked he was when he became a Christian and his own mother violently rejected his conversion. They'd always been devoted and loyal to each other. But when he told her he'd become a Christian, his sweet, gentle mother said, "Don't ever mention the name of Jesus again in this house. Go to your room." Ron was crushed because he'd been so secure in their relationship that he hadn't anticipated this reaction at all. But sometimes rejection is actually a timing problem.

You have to give people time to understand what you're doing when you introduce a new element into an established relationship. Ron's mother eventually became a

Christian herself, and today she enthusiastically supports him in everything he's doing with his life. But every transition takes time and patience.

It's important not to let negative vibrations in a relationship shake your confidence in yourself. It may be only temporary. When people love you, they'll make room for what's important to you, and eventually they'll come to understand it. Meanwhile, even if their rejection shakes you up, just make sure it doesn't shake you loose!

3. IT FEEDS YOUR NATURAL INSECURITY. Great men and women who've accomplished amazing feats often admit they have a core of insecurity. It's true of everybody. The difference is that great men and women persist and pursue their dreams in spite of their insecurity. When people reject your ideas or laugh at what you're doing, it feeds that natural insecurity we all have. But it's your decision at that point. You can surrender to it and give up your dreams, or you can fight back and win!

4. IT CRACKS YOUR CONFIDENCE. Let's say you're sailing along, building a business, pursuing a dream, and suddenly somebody hits you in a vulnerable spot. "I don't believe in you. I don't like what you're doing. I think you're wrong, wrong, wrong!" If you take that hit to heart, your ego will weaken and your confidence will crack.

A Michigan and Kentucky basketball game was tied, and it was going into overtime. The Kentucky Wildcats began to drive for the win. Then with a four-point lead, Wildcat Jamal Mashburn, the leading scorer, rebounder, and heart and soul of the team, fouled out with twenty-six points. Kentucky's confidence cracked. Something happened to their flow, their rhythm. They became tentative and hesitant. They no longer drove the ball inside; they no longer went for layups or tried to draw a foul. The passion and intensity were gone. Michigan came back and took the lead, winning the game by three points in overtime.

That's what a lack of confidence can do to you. Maybe you're doing great, then suddenly, you get hit with a personal rejection when you're not looking. Your confidence cracks. You may still be building your business and developing your dream, but your rhythm, your style, is missing. And you wonder why things are slowing down. The truth is you've got a doubt inside because you believed the rejection of the rejecter.

This is vital. When somebody rejects you, that's the time to get more aggressive, not less. That's the time to go faster, go farther. That's the time to redouble your belief in yourself. I remember when anybody rejected me in the early days of my business, I'd be very gracious to them. It's important to be courteous and gracious with people, even if they're rejecting you. But as soon as I got outside, I'd say inside myself, "You're going to eat them words, baby! I'm going to find two better than you and put them where you would have been!"

See, I knew I couldn't afford to let my ego get fractured. I couldn't afford to let my confidence crack. There was too much at stake. Later on down the line, if there was any validity in what the rejecter said, I might take a look at it and make adjustments. But that had to be *later*. At the time of the rejection, I had to get stronger, not weaker.

5. IT ATTACKS YOUR MOST BASIC MOTIVATION. It's when people question your motives that rejection hurts most. You can handle most of the flack they give you until you hear someone say, "You're greedy. You're materialistic. You're manipulating other people." That's when the sting hits the core of your heart, especially when the one who's saying it is someone you love, someone you'd thought would know you better than that.

Here's the test of your guts, your leadership, your soul: Are you going to go on and build your dream even when they're questioning your motives, or are you going to give in to emotional blackmail?

One young couple told me that the husband's parents were creating havoc in their marriage by their continual verbal barrages and controlling maneuvers. "They've attacked our dreams and slandered our motivation and told us we were wrong and selfish." Essentially, the parents were saying to this couple, "If you don't do what we want you to do, then we're going to judge you, evaluate you, and use every emotional pressure we can to control you."

After some serious counseling time, that couple determined to break the yoke of that emotional blackmail. They loved their parents and wanted a good relationship with them, but they realized they had to be adults and make their own decisions about their future. It took courage to stand firm when the emotional pressure was on, but they did it.

You have to develop courage if you're going to deal with rejection successfully. Commit to your own values, your own beliefs, your own dreams. It's not easy, but without it you'll never have what you want most in life—and you'll never become who you could have been.

How *Not* to Respond to Rejection
Let me warn you of a few ways people respond to rejection that defeat them in the long run. If you're having any of these reactions, you may want to take a different tack.

1. RAPID RETREAT. It may sound blunt, but this is a coward's response. When cowards are criticized, they quit. Retreating is the fastest way to lose both your dignity and your dreams.

2. SELLOUT TO SELF-DOUBT. Don't ever believe in the opposition more than you believe in yourself. When people criticize you, it's vital not to sell out to their point of view.

Every great leader has to plow through opposition and ridicule in order to achieve a dream. When Abraham Lincoln became active in politics and ran for the presidency, newspapers around the country called him "the old baboon" and "that ape, Abraham Lincoln."

Ulysses S. Grant had a reputation for alcoholism and gruffness. When he was first appointed lieutenant general, he came to the White House in very simple clothing with mud on his boots. All the elite, socially correct men and women of the administration in Washington looked at him with disbelief. Could this be U. S. Grant?

Look at history and read the stories. Alexander the Great was told he was too young. Julius Caesar was considered too old. Napoleon was from the wrong side of the tracks. It's a simple fact that all great leaders face rejection. But no matter how intense the opposition, there's one thing they have in common: *They don't sell out to self-doubt and abandon their dreams.*

3. CAMOUFLAGED COMPROMISE. When you've had a taste of success, there's a dangerous reaction to criticism that I've seen happen again and again. It's a subtle attitude of compromise. You don't want to alienate the people who are criticizing you, but you don't want to give up either. So you decide not to go for the whole win, but to make it look as though you are—even to yourself.

In the networking business, we call those people "functioneers." A functioneer is someone who attends numerous functions, loves them, seems to be working toward his or her dream—and yet the dream never comes true. Why? Because the functioneer is holding back just enough to avoid risking too much disapproval.

Camouflaged compromise means that you won't get results—but you'll sure look like you're trying.

4. APPROVAL PURSUIT. Some people purposely go after the approval of people who are rejecting them. They seek to "win over" those who disapprove of what they're doing. Ron confided to me that this was one of his own greatest challenges. "I want people to like me, and I'm sensitive to rejection, so I constantly have to overcome my need to pursue approval. I found helpful what Walter Isaacson said in his biography of Henry Kissinger: 'Kissinger responded to critics with too much intensity and wasted enormous amounts of energy, time, and force of heart in trying to convince people who had already rejected him.' "

This is an easy trap to fall into. But the truth is, you don't need to try to "win over" those who are not on your side. The best thing you can do for yourself—and for them— is to build a successful business anyway. Just remember: *When you seek people's approval too much, you lose their respect.*

5. BECOMING A TURTLE. This is a tendency to tighten up and go inside your shell for protection. It breeds bitterness and noncommunication. It also keeps you from achieving any kind of success. If you stay inside your shell, your rejecter has won.

6. RECYCLING THE REJECTION. You kick me; I kick the dog. That's recycled rejection. Someone hurts your feelings, so you lash out at someone else to release the negative emotions. That's self-defeating and only breaks down your alliances with people around you. Your recycled rejection will cost you more than the original one.

7. REJECTION REFLECTION. You may be tempted to go into an introspective mode after an experience of rejection, especially if that's your personality style anyway. Avoid that temptation. It will immobilize you. I've never

seen rejection-triggered introspection produce anything positive. It just drains you of energy and takes you out of the game.

Right Ways to Respond to Rejection

Here are five things you need to develop that will help you deal with rejection successfully.

1. SPIRITUAL CLARITY. When Jesus Christ came into my life, spiritual clarity occurred.

Whether or not you believe in Jesus Christ, you need spiritual clarity. You must settle the basic debate of right and wrong. Otherwise you can be shaken by rejection because you will not be sure if what you're doing is right or wrong.

2. BATTLE TRAINING. During the Civil War, the officers of the Federal army were excited when they heard new units were coming to help fight the Battle of Chickamauga Creek. But General William Sherman, who commanded the troops, knew the background of the new recruits. "Boys," he said, "this is not what you hoped for, because we have more bodies, but they'll be almost useless. They have no battle training."

Sherman proved to be correct. In the heat of battle, the new men would break and run, not because they were cowards but because they didn't know what to do. As the war progressed, though, these same men became battle trained and hardened. They became some of the best troops in the army.

If you're to overcome rejection, you need "battle training" too. It comes from several sources:

a. *From warriors who know how to win.* Listen to people who have made it to the place you want to be. They know how to do it. Let their advice guide you and give you wisdom as you deal with the same thing they did.

b. *From battle reading.* Do "battle reading" in your particular areas of weakness on a regular basis. Read your Bible and positive motivational books. Find whatever builds your backbone and use it. Battle readiness is a mentality, an attitude—plus accurate information. Leaders are readers.

c. *From personal experience.* Get out there and practice what you've learned from your mentors. Don't become a professional student while other people are out there laying hold of the prize. In the game of life, success breeds success, and failures breed success too—as long as you put into practice what you're learning and don't give up.

3. A LOVE OF EXCELLENCE. Winners respect excellence. Conversely, they disrespect mediocrity and laziness. You need to develop an immunity to the criticism of those whose lifestyles and values you do not respect. If you don't admire the person, why should their criticism affect you?

Having a love of excellence also means you learn lessons from rejecters. Sometimes there's an element of truth in what they're saying, and you can learn from it, but *never* at the time of the rejection. That's when you need to be strong and decisively nonreflective. But later you can take whatever nugget of validity may be there and use it to move you further toward your goals.

I remember a guy who criticized the ring I was wearing when I first got started in the business. It was my high school ring, and he thought it wasn't classy enough to represent my business. I knew enough not to let the criticism get to me. I just explained to him that the ring had personal meaning to me because of the history it represented. But later on, I decided there was some value in what he was saying. I bought myself a diamond ring and invested it with personal meaning about my future, instead of my past. That new ring became a symbol of where I was going, not where I had been.

4. TRUE GRIT. If you react to rejection properly, you will become a leader.

When a pastor asked Ron what to do about the opposition and rejection he felt from his congregation, Ron told him wisely: "Love them. Pray for them. And be thankful you've got an opportunity to become a pioneer with backbone and discipline who can lead the way."

I say "Amen" to that!

True grit is what you've got to develop if you're going to win big. It means courage to stick with your purpose against all odds. It doesn't mean harshness or hard-hearted toughness. It means respecting yourself and others enough that you can say, "Hey, this may not be your dream, but it's mine, and I *will* do it." Ultimately, there's no greater secret of success than true grit.

True grit gives you three things:

a. *Emotional control.* You don't give in to depression, anxiety, fear, or guilt.

b. *Mental discipline.* You don't allow yourself to dwell on the negative; instead you focus on positive experiences.

c. *The power of chosen optimism.* You can choose to be optimistic. You don't allow rejection to spoil you, control you, or push you into retreat.

Ultimately, rejection is actually good for you. It teaches you to focus on your dreams and gives you the opportunity to choose your attitude and your priorities. It gives you the strength to be a leader and an example to others. As you face combat, you develop the discipline to win.

Get a Grip on Your Ego

Learning how to work with people will be hard if your ego is out of whack. But if you get a grip on your ego and learn to operate with humility, you'll go further than you ever thought you could go.

One of the biggest roadblocks to working with people is found in the ego department. Recently I was with one of the most successful businessmen I know, and he made a comment I believe is true. He said, "This decade is going to be the greatest one our network has ever seen. But we've got one problem. I've been around for a long time, and the biggest thing that can derail our people is if their egos get out of control. The one thing that can protect our success is a strong dose of humility."

How's Your Ego Doing?

A healthy ego is a fine thing. You've got to have a strong sense of your own value and identity to create anything in life. But an overactive ego can sabotage your work. Most people with ego problems don't even know they have them. That's why egos can be so hazardous.

So here are a few signs that will help you check up on yourself. Don't get discouraged if you relate to some of these. It's much better to realize it and begin to deal with it than to go on damaging your business and your relationships without even knowing what's happening.

1. YOU FEEL SECRETLY HURT OR RESENTFUL WHEN OTHER PEOPLE ARE RECOGNIZED OR REWARDED. How do you react when someone else gets recognition and you don't? Are you always sensitive to whether or not you are getting the recognition you deserve? If so, then it's going to be hard to relate to people without being easily offended by their humanness. It's a simple fact that very few people notice everything you do for them. It's not that they're calloused or rude. They're just so caught up in their own feelings and circumstances that they're not tuned in to everything else.

When your ego is healthy, you do things for people because you want to do it and you like the result. Naturally, you enjoy recognition too. But seeing other people succeed is actually the best reward.

2. YOU TEND TO RESIST NEW INFORMATION. When we close our minds to new ideas, it's a sign that we've decided we know everything we need to know. I don't think anybody does this consciously. It would be too absurd to say you already know everything. But an overactive ego causes us to stop actively listening and learning.

It could be we're afraid our ideas will be challenged, or maybe we're afraid we'll be proven wrong about something. Maybe we just get mentally lazy sometimes. Whatever it is, it's dangerous, because when we stop learning and growing, we start to repel people. We also start to stagnate—which is the beginning of failure.

One of the great businessmen of our time, Sam Walton, used to go into competitors' stores and watch what they did in order to learn from them. One day, Jack Shoemaker, former president of Wal-Mart stores, accompanied Sam on such a visit. The particular store they visited was a disaster. Shoemaker walked around the aisles thinking, "Sam can't learn anything from this place. It's awful." The aisles were cluttered, the shelves were a shambles, and the service was terrible. But even in that chaos, Sam Walton found one tiny thing on a shelf that looked good. He said, "Jack, look at this. That's great. Why aren't we doing that?" You know what Sam Walton had? He had humility. That's why he was at the top. He never lost his humility. He stayed teachable.

It's vital to have an attitude of humility and a willingness to learn from anybody if you're going to reach high goals in your life—and keep on reaching them.

3. YOU TALK ABOUT YOURSELF TOO MUCH. "Let another praise you, and not your own mouth." That's real good advice from Proverbs 27:2 in the Bible. Have you been around people who talk about themselves constantly—"I said this. I said that. I did this. I did that."—until you get tired of hearing it?

Some people take every conversation and turn it into another story about themselves. That's a symptom of an unhealthy ego. So if you catch yourself talking too much about your own stuff—whether it's goals or achievements or conversations or experiences—beware. You may be alienating people without knowing it. Back up. Tune in to whom you're talking and find out what they have to say. Listen more than you talk. It'll keep your ego on the right track.

4. YOU TEND TO DE-EDIFY OTHER PEOPLE. When you talk about other people, what do you say? Do you always talk about them with deep respect and admiration? Or do you tend to be critical? Analytical? De-edifying? To de-edify people is to tear them down instead of building them up.

Gossip is a subtle thing. It's not usually a conscious attack. It's more of a negative analysis of someone—not meant to harm, of course. But the fact is, it always does. Unhealthy egos tend to take critical and analytical positions more than healthy ones. They see the flaws in people—and they usually discuss them.

In religious circles, de-edification can come in the form of concerned conversation and prayer about someone else's "struggles." In other circles, it may show up as a sort of sarcastic humor, a disrespectful joking that wins laughter at the expense of another person's dignity.

The Bible says that if we have a problem with someone, we're to deal with it personally, face-to-face, and try to set things right. It also speaks strongly against gossip and "backbiting," an old term that means tearing others down behind their backs.

Why do we put other people down? Most of the time it's just ego trying to look good in comparison with someone else. Sometimes we like the attention we get when we're clever at insulting someone—a form of disrespect made fashionable today by TV sitcoms.

But whatever the reason, de-edification in any form demonstrates that the person doing it considers himself or herself to be worthy of judging someone else. This is the ultimate ego trip.

5. YOU RESIST CONSTRUCTIVE FEEDBACK. You've probably heard the humorous expression, "I've got my mind made up. Don't confuse me with the facts!" That's the

overactive ego speaking. It doesn't like to be proven wrong and will go to great lengths to avoid it. People with ego problems will tend to disregard the truth in favor of maintaining their already established beliefs about something. That's why they're not good at receiving input from other people—even when that input would help them.

We never know as much as we think we know. And there are always blind spots in whatever work we do. That's why we need the input of other people if we're going to perform at our best. But an unhealthy ego will obstruct that. You'll find yourself being intimidated by or resisting other people's helpful comments. You have to get a grip on your ego if you're going to benefit from other people's input.

6. YOU TREAT THE LAWS OF GOD LIGHTLY. One of the most serious symptoms of a problem ego is when you start to treat God's laws with disrespect. If you find yourself cheating, breaking the rules, violating the rights of other people, and acting like the world exists only for you—these are sure signs you've lost touch with the reality of who you are.

Sometimes, when we get a little taste of success, we start thinking God's rules don't apply to us anymore. After all, we're special, aren't we? We've succeeded, haven't we? Some of the most blatant sinners are rich and powerful people whose position has made them feel invulnerable.

But the Bible says, "Be sure that your sin will find you out" (Numbers 32:23). And "the wages of sin is death, but the gift of God is eternal life in Christ Jesus our Lord" (Romans 6:23). Why do I say this in a book about people skills and success in business? Because it's a vital part of the success picture. The fact is, if you treat the laws of God lightly, you'll pay a horrendous price. But if you respect them and build your life around them, your success will be permanent and your joy, full.

How to Retain Humility

So how do we keep egos under control? I've learned to keep mine in balance by following just a few simple guidelines.

1. NEVER LOSE YOUR SENSE OF WONDER AT WHAT YOU'RE LEARNING FROM OTHERS. We can learn from absolutely everybody. I love to hear Diamonds talk about what they've experienced. I can always learn something new from them. But I learn from non-Diamonds too. I'm constantly open to whatever I can gain from their conversation. I can even learn from their failures and mistakes. I never take for granted the wisdom I find in others.

2. CULTIVATE GRATEFULNESS. A sweet, wonderful woman of prayer once said, "The greatest protection against arrogance in life is maintaining a sincere gratitude toward God." This is true. A man I know once asked me how I kept from becoming proud and egotistical in light of the wealth I've gained over the years. "It isn't hard," I told him, "when you start every day of your life on your face before the One who made you." Gratitude toward God will insulate you against both the pressures of the world—and an inflated sense of your own accomplishments. It will make you more aware of your responsibilities than your achievements.

3. PRAY FOR A GIVING ATTITUDE. True leaders are always givers. If you want to be a great leader, Jesus said you'll have to become the servant of everyone. So ask God to give you a servant spirit. He'll be happy to answer that prayer. But be prepared to grow! And get ready to give up your overinvolvement with yourself.

4. MAKE PEOPLE YOUR PRIORITY. There's a saying, "Love people and use things. Don't use people and love things." People are the crown of God's creation. They are His joy, His treasures. They are more important than any possession or achievement. Always keep in your mind how precious people are to God, and ask Him to help you see them clearly. It's not hard to keep your ego in line when you're constantly thinking about the welfare of others.

5. LEARN TO SEE YOURSELF FROM GOD'S PERSPECTIVE. God loves you—yes, *you*—dearly. You're a priceless treasure to Him. When you're secure in the love of God, you don't need to puff yourself up in order to feel important. You can relax. Ego problems always come from fear—fear of not being important enough.

Once you realize and experience the love of God on the inside of you, nothing stays the same. Everything is different. You can be yourself and begin to care about other people, knowing how precious each of us is to Him. You start to outgrow your fears and be confident that God really is making you into the beautiful person He knows you to be.

When you see yourself in the light of God, you can see your own flaws and weaknesses. You see how far you have to go in living up to His great and loving character. It's not hard to keep your ego in line when you're comparing yourself with God's awesomeness—instead of other people's flaws.

Humility is a vital part of relating successfully to people. Without it, you won't get very far. With it, you can go as far up the ladder of success as you want to go. And what's more, you're going to take many, many people with you along the way.

Eliminate Negative Patterns

Do you know someone who constantly overreacts? Or who's always gruff and mean—toward everyone? Have you ever experienced competitive friction with a coworker or a family member, even when you're consciously trying to get along with them? If so, then you've been on the receiving end of someone else's negative patterns.

Negative Relationship Patterns

Chances are you've got a few negative patterns of your own. It's important to recognize them for what they are: habits that can damage and even destroy relationships. Here are a few I've noticed over the years. If you recognize yourself in any of these, it's time to make some adjustments.

Temperamentalism

Over the years I've heard people with bad tempers say, "I've always been this way. I've always had a temper. It's just the way I am." That's an irresponsible approach to something that needs changing. These people don't want to take responsibility for their own temperament. Instead of working to correct an aspect of their personality that hurts other people, they want to claim immunity by heredity.

But that's not the way it is. Everybody has a choice. In fact, you got the way you are by making choices, day after day. And you can become whatever you want to be by making new choices, day by day. It's that simple. I didn't say it's *easy*. I said it's *simple*.

Nobody is a slave to his own temperament. Whatever dominant personality type you were born with, you can still make changes. You don't need to run roughshod over other people and then defend yourself by saying you're just "blunt" or "hard driving." You can learn to relate to people with kindness. It's inside you, it really is. You just have to learn to bring it out.

I know of one corporate CEO who had a reputation for a "nuclear" style when things weren't going his way—he blew through like a hydrogen bomb, wiping out everybody who got in his line of fire. Down the line, however, he changed. An interviewer from *Fortune* magazine commented at one point, "An amazing transformation has occurred. He's still a driver, still intense, but he's learned to work with people."

If you have problems with your temperament, you need to recognize the need for adjustment on your part if you're going to get along with other people. Do you want to succeed in business and in life? Then don't give in to temperamentalism. After all, what is genuine maturity? It's developing skill in areas of life where you recognize you need to change. Immaturity is stubbornly clinging to your old habits and insisting other people adjust to you.

Response laziness
I know people who love to spout off whatever they think without considering the consequences. In fact, I asked one

of them once why he felt the freedom to slam people. He said, "I'm just being honest. I tell them what I think, and it feels great." That's the core problem of response laziness. It feels great—temporarily—to instantly vent whatever response is boiling around on the inside. But it's actually a lazy thing to do. As in all laziness, giving in to a momentary release never produces what you really want in the long run.

Obviously, it's harder to take the time and develop the skill to explain to someone why you think what you think and to say it in a way they can relate to. It's much easier to just let go and take verbal swings at people whenever you feel like it. But if you want powerful relationships with strong and loyal ties, it's vital to learn to think before you respond to people. You need to evaluate how your words are going to come across. When you don't, you'll pay a price you hadn't counted on paying. And it will always be too high.

Reaction ruts

Once you've started reacting in a certain way to certain people or situations, it's tempting to repeat that habit pattern every time. Instead of maintaining a fresh perspective, you fall into the old "knee-jerk" reaction you've had so many times before. It's become a reflex. A reaction rut. Maybe you decided years ago to be mad at a certain person because he mistreated you or somebody you loved. Now whenever you see that person (or anyone who reminds you of that person), you go into an automatic "mad."

Some married couples have almost identical arguments over and over again for exactly this reason. They've established emotional programs—like computer programs. They hit some predictable emotional switch, and it starts running. Same argument, one more time. Until these couples stop and take a look at what they're doing, they'll never really connect with each other, much less resolve the argument.

Every one of us has programs like that filed away in the back of our mind. Hit a certain trigger, and we respond like puppets. The program's been engaged. In order to break out of this mechanical response pattern, we need to reprogram the program. We need to realize we have an opportunity to be with a flesh-and-blood wife, son, daughter, business associate, or friend and to learn to respond to each person individually, from the heart.

Relational fantasies

Sometimes you have to face the fact that a person is doing what he or she is doing or that a situation is how it is. It doesn't help to cling to magical thinking—supposing that someone will miraculously change and start treating you the way you want just because you want them to. That kind of thinking is fantasy. And it keeps you from doing what really needs to be done.

Some situations simply will not work, no matter how hard you try to make them work. You have to look reality in the eye. You have to deal with people where they actually are. Maybe they don't want a relationship with you. Be realistic about that. You can only work with the truth, not some fantasy of the situation. Maybe your greatest dream has been to have a good relationship with someone you love, but it hasn't worked. It's possible to build a good relationship and work with difficult situations, but you can't pretend the situation is anything other than what it is. Personal honesty is the first step in developing the skills to move any relationship in a positive direction.

Operating from assumptions, not facts

Think for a moment about how irritating it is to have someone tell you what you're thinking or feeling, or why you've done something. Doesn't it make you mad when someone assumes he or she has the power to read your thoughts or motives?

The truth is no one really knows what you're thinking except you. Likewise, it's not smart to assume you know what anyone else is thinking without checking with them. It's always good to clarify and define things—just so no one jumps to any inaccurate conclusions.

An elementary school teacher was reviewing vocabulary words with her students. She asked, "Does anyone know what the word *pause* means?" One little girl raised her hand and said, "It's the button you push when you want your VCR to wait." That wasn't the answer the teacher was expecting, but it was that little girl's interpretation of *pause* according to her own experience.

That kind of thing happens in every relationship. When I hear you say something, I'm going to interpret it according to my own experience. If we don't clarify what you're saying and what I'm hearing, I may miss your point entirely and not even know it!

That's why you've got to take this matter of assumptions seriously. If you don't, you'll build up barriers and bitterness. Be especially careful to check your assumptions with people you know well. You're more likely to assume you know what your spouse thinks or what your business associate would want done in a certain situation, than you are someone you know less intimately. The problem is that you could be entirely wrong. I've discovered you have to nail things down with great precision if you're going to avoid dangerous and destructive misunderstandings.

Recently some men were involved in a building project at my house. Our relationship became strained because I thought I had communicated what I wanted done, and they were totally convinced I had said something different. Finally, we had a positive, open conversation and realized we'd had a breakdown in communication.

Remember this: Assumption is assassination. If you operate on the basis of assumptions, you'll leave behind you a trail of misunderstandings that will create strain in all your relationships.

Pouring negatives onto others

Most of us know it's not good to take out our tension on other people, but a lot of times we do it anyway. It's so easy to "take it out on the family" when something's gone wrong at work or there are frustrations facing us in business. But the only possible result of this kind of action is to spoil the relationship with someone who has absolutely nothing to do with the situation. Why should we pour our troubles all over the people who could be our best support?

Recently I spoke with a lady in her seventies who said sadly, "My kids don't want to come around anymore." After spending some time with her myself, I knew why! She was filled with negative statements. Although I didn't excuse the children for neglecting their mother, I knew the negative climate she'd created made it difficult for people to enjoy being around her.

Do you want to wind up like that? If you don't, you'd better determine to practice positives instead of negatives. And when someone else dumps his or her negatives all over you, determine to listen with kindness and empathy. *But don't ever join in the negativity, even if it seems legitimate.* The last thing a negative person needs is agreement. Instead, love, listen, and understand. Encourage a positive perspective, but don't expect the person to change his or her point of view while you're sitting there. Give that person time to process your input. Negative programs in people don't change overnight. But they will change eventually—if you don't give up.

Manipulation games

Manipulation is a way of getting what you want from someone without laying all the cards on the table. It's a form of disrespect that says, in essence, "I've already decided that what I want is good for you, so I'll do whatever is necessary to get you to do what I want."

Manipulators often love the people they manipulate in a warped sort of way. They love you, but they withhold their approval until you come around to their way of thinking. They can be very sweet and appear to really care for your welfare—as long as they are getting what they want from you.

Most manipulators are not fully aware they're doing it. So how can you know if you're the one doing the manipulating? Ask yourself this question: *When I'm with this person, do we always wind up doing what I want to do? Do I ever disregard what the other person wants? And if we argue, do I always win?* These are indicators that you've probably picked up the art of manipulation. The sooner you put it down and give others equal power in the relationship, the better for everyone.

Attack of the raptor

Ron shared a story that illustrates the raptor. He said that in Steven Spielberg's classic movie *Jurassic Park,* Dr. Allen Grant explains how the dinosaur Velociraptor attacks. A raptor walks over and looks you in the face, appearing to be friendly, while two other raptors, unseen by you, are sneaking up on either side. When the right moment occurs, the raptors move in, slash their victim with their retractable razorlike claws, and eat him on the spot. The remarkable thing is that the raptor looks so friendly in the beginning of the encounter, but in the end, it's deadly.

Over the last few years, psychologists and sociologists who've probed into American life have discovered tremendous reservoirs of anger in people. Although they're not certain why this is occurring, they know that on any given day, people experience major frustrations—their anger boiling beneath the surface, ready to erupt. Because they know they need to get along with people, they try to be friendly and nice on the surface. However, if the moment presents itself, they can go instantly on the offensive.

Obviously, you wouldn't consciously use a friendly exterior to lure someone into a trap. But if you have anger hiding beneath your amiable appearance, it's extremely hazardous to your relationships. You need to find a way to resolve this anger—reducing your frustrations through better organization of your time, getting some counseling, or maybe just getting more rest. No matter how you look at it, relationships are hard to maintain when people are afraid of sudden outbursts or lurking hostility.

Changing Negative Patterns

If you notice any of these behavior patterns showing up in your life on occasion, don't get discouraged. It only means one thing: You're human. Human beings aren't perfect. But the great thing is we have the power to change. Once you decide that relationships are more important than catering to old habits and immediate impulses, you can make some creative changes in your life. In fact, I'll be bold enough to say that your deepest dreams will never come true until you're willing to make big changes in these areas. But let me warn you about some things:

Don't be trapped by perfectionism

It's vital to learn the difference between striving for excellence and demanding perfection. That's true of yourself and everybody else, too. People aren't perfect. I had to smile when one man told me he wanted to have sex "just right" with his wife. I told him I didn't think there was a "just right" way to have sex. There's just sex, and you enjoy it. You love each other and enjoy the experience of being together.

Perfectionism says, "If you can't do it perfectly, get out of the game." Excellence says, "Go at it one more time, you're getting better."

Aiming at excellence is a good thing—in every area of life. But always trying to be perfect is really a form of fear. It's a way of saying, "I'm afraid if I don't do something flawlessly, I'm no good." Perfectionism grows in the soil of insecurity. In fact, in that soil even excellence can't grow. Fear kills excellence. In fact, fear kills just about everything that's good.

So don't let perfectionism rob you of the beautiful changes you can have in your life. Just determine to take one step at a time. When you mess up, go at it again. It's taken you a few years to get the way you are today, and it may take you a little while to get skillful at your new thinking and behavior patterns. But you'll make it. In fact, you'll get better every day if you just keep working at it. Excellence is a wonderful and endless pursuit that will take you as far as you want to go, one step at a time.

Don't ignore your vulnerabilities

Since we're all human, we all have weak points. There's nothing wrong with that. It's how we're built. The only thing we need to do is make sure we take those weak points into account. Don't overlook them. Take care of them.

When one of my distributors told me, "I'm working so hard, and I'm starting to make a lot of mistakes," I asked him simply, "When was the last time you took a break? When have you had some private time with God or had an evening with your wife?" He shook his head and said, "I haven't had time for that." I told him seriously that he couldn't afford not to have time for that. I reminded him that all winners learn how to pace themselves. They understand when they need a reward and when they need to relax. A winner takes care of his own vulnerabilities.

Alcoholics Anonymous has a phrase I like. They call it the HALT warning system. They say you're most vulnerable to becoming upset when you are:

- Hungry
- Angry
- Lonely
- Tired

During those times, we're more vulnerable to our own weaknesses. Alcoholics are more prone to drink during those times. Food-a-holics are more prone to eat. People in stressed marriages are more prone to affairs when those times hit. That's why it's important not to share your needs with a man or woman outside your marriage whenever you're hungry, tired, lonely, and/or mad at your spouse for any reason.

The important thing is to take responsibility for taking care of yourself. Don't add to your own stress by pushing it past the limits you know you have. When you're hungry, angry, lonely, or tired, *stop*. Take care of the vulnerability. *Then*, go on.

One other thing to avoid

When you're vulnerable, don't go find someone as miserable, lonely, or angry as you are and join up with them. It's really tempting, when you're in a vulnerable place, to look for agreement and support from people who feel just like you do. But that's *not* who you need to spend time with. In fact, the opposite is true. When you're vulnerable is the most important time to hook up with people who are stronger than you are at the moment. So when you're feeling weak, avoid two kinds of people: people who share your weaknesses and people who criticize them. Neither group is good for you. Get with some people who are strong and understanding. Only listen to people you trust—people who actually have your best interests at heart and who live the way you want to live.

Turning Negative Patterns into Positive Ones

How do you do it? How do you take the negative habits you've had for years and begin to turn them in a positive direction? It's not really that hard. You just:

- Recognize the specific "skill killers" you've been using in your own life.
- Realize the negative ways these things have been affecting you and your relationships.
- Understand you don't have to give in to negative patterns; you can still choose.
- Ask God and a few people you trust for help in keeping you accountable as you chip away at the "skill killers," one by one.
- Keep moving ahead with relationships, not being afraid to make mistakes while you're growing in your people skills.

Gather up your courage and choose one "skill killer" to begin on. Within a short while, you'll be amazed at the difference removing even one of these negative patterns will make in your life!

PART Three

Understanding Who You Are

Choosing Your View of Human Nature

I believe there are two different ways of looking at the world and at human nature. You may not agree with this point of view, but Ron and I feel it explains so much. Whatever perspective you choose, I believe it will radically affect your relationships with people and how you interact with them.

How you understand people is important. We've spent several chapters talking about knocking the negatives out of our lives. But if you don't understand why people do what they do, you don't really understand them at all. And if you don't understand them, you'll be constantly impatient and frustrated with them instead of being kind and in control of the situation.

Obviously, human behavior is a subject that's complex enough to write volumes about. What I'm saying in this chapter is a basic introduction, a bird's-eye view of two entirely different ways of understanding people—the Christian view and the humanistic view. I believe if you see exactly what is being said by whom, sort it out, and think it through, then you can make a decision as to which way of thinking you believe is right.

The Christian view of people understands them in the light of their relationship to God, while the humanistic view essentially leaves God out of the picture. I'm sure you've already realized from our discussions in previous chapters that the dynamic people skills Ron and I are teaching grow out of our own Christian perspective. We approach the subject of human nature from a biblical perspective. We don't want to offend anyone who does not share this belief because we deeply respect your right to choose your personal perspective in life. However, we believe that how you choose to see things in this arena will affect the way you relate to people— including yourself—in every situation.

Looking at these two basic views of human nature is a great opportunity to review your own perspective. As I outline the basics of these two systems of thought, again, from my perspective, why don't you look carefully to see not only what you think or what you believe but also how you actually operate in your everyday life? Because how you operate *is* what you believe, whether you realize it or not.

The Humanistic View of People

1. LIFE IS PRIMARILY A PHYSICAL PHENOMENON. The humanistic view is built on an assumption that there is no spiritual dimension to life. Human life and nature aren't seen with any reference to a God-being. This perspective considers this tangible life to be all there is; all of human knowledge and experience is bound up within this framework. Moreover, there is not true spiritual knowledge or experience. What some people think to be spiritual experience is actually a collection of different ideas, thoughts, physical sensations, reactions, and emotions.

2. PEOPLE ARE SIMPLY AN ADVANCED FORM OF
ANIMAL LIFE. If there is no God, then another explanation
is needed for human existence. One of the most popular
humanistic theories is the theory of mechanistic evolution,
also called philosophical Darwinism. In its extreme form,
that theory holds that life was generated accidentally
through a series of spontaneous coincidences. Everything
that exists, from the human eye to the circulatory system,
from the power of our brain waves to the way the planet
rotates on its axis—is presumed to be an accident. Not a
result of intelligent design, but of coincidence. Since human
beings are very complex organisms, this theory proposes
that we must have developed from less complex organisms.
In other words, we're advanced animals living in a strictly
material universe.

Although the theory of evolution is often taught as
scientific fact, for many people it's become a theory to
explain the origin of the world in the context of a nonexistent
God. The truth is, no one can prove that God does not exist,
any more than they can prove that every species of life
developed through a series of mutations. I'm told researchers
are now expressing serious skepticism over various theories
of evolution because there are giant gaps and unanswered
questions. For me, it's a bigger stretch of faith to believe that
human life, as well as the entire universe, accidentally
evolved, than to believe that some extremely intelligent
Being created it.

3. PEOPLE ARE MORALLY NEUTRAL. If people are seen
without reference to God, there's no common standard of
truth or values outside ourselves. This makes us morally
neutral creatures. We do whatever suits us according to our
own experiences and understanding. There's no legitimate

moral standard or reference point for what is right and wrong.

This view excuses certain behaviors that, from my own personal standpoint as a Christian, are in violation of the laws of God in the Bible. But in a humanistic context, values are a personal thing. People just make up their own rules.

4. PEOPLE ARE ENVIRONMENTALLY CONTROLLED AND DEVELOPED. The humanistic view says we're basically a product of our social, psychological, and moral environment. Since God isn't taken into account, people are seen primarily as biological creatures, our experience of life made up of our reactions and responses to our environment. We can't really "rise above" our environment since there is no spiritual part of us to do that.

5. PEOPLE ARE NATURALLY CAPABLE OF UNLIMITED IMPROVEMENT. From the humanistic perspective, if people are products of their environment, then it follows that proper education and training will produce better and better people. As Christians, we also believe there's value in good education and training. But the humanist view holds that there is nothing standing in our way. Humanists believe we're naturally capable of unlimited improvement because there's no such thing as "sin" to hold us back. Social engineering, then, is the whole answer to the human dilemma. The way to deal with violence, war, conflict, hatred, and killing is to educate it out of us.

That's a nice idea, but is it true? Every prison has criminals in it with brilliant and highly educated minds. If it's a fact that highly educated people can still be evil— there must be a deeper problem, one that the humanistic philosophy doesn't acknowledge.

The Christian View of People

The Christian view has its basis in the Bible in the first three chapters of Genesis, which is part of the shared heritage of Jews and Christians. It presents the historical origin of the universe and the human race. We believe it to be fact. It doesn't take long to read it, so if you can put your hands on a Bible, you can check it out for yourself.

1. PEOPLE ARE CREATED IN GOD'S IMAGE. The first words in the Bible are "In the beginning, God created." According to the biblical account, God made us. And He made us like Himself. This refers not just to our physical bodies but to all the characteristics that make people unique among living creatures—our capacity for language, concepts, understanding, commitment, dreams, faith, and relationships. All of these are characteristics common to both God and us.

Some people think of God as an invention of the human mind. But the Bible says we're actually an invention of His mind! He's not our idea; we were His! Every one of us bears His imprint on the very deepest part of ourselves. This perspective causes us to see people as very significant. Each one is a priceless being designed by God and precious to Him. So how we treat each person is important.

Realizing we're made in God's image opens up incredible possibilities for personal growth and change. As we discover the characteristics of God—such as perfect love, justice, kindness—we realize we can become more loving, fair, and kind, too. After all, it's who we really are.

2. WE'RE A FLAWED CREATION. According to the Bible, the human story isn't entirely a rosy picture, as anyone can see from watching the news. The world is full of evil—and this comes from the evil in the human heart—pride, envy, selfishness, deceit, laziness, power abuse. Genesis tells how all that got started; the first man and woman broke up

their perfect fellowship with God by listening to the lie of their archenemy, Satan.

It was that broken relationship with God, what the Bible calls "sin," that brought about spiritual death and a sinful nature that's part of the human condition. Sin also brought a curse of disease, difficulty, and disaster on human life. Evil and sin are part of everyone's life in that no one lives up to the ideal for which they were created.

3. GOD MADE RECOVERY POSSIBLE. Just because people rebelled against God didn't mean God abandoned His original purpose. Far from it! In fact, the whole story of the Bible is the story of God's work in bringing people back to Himself. The bottom line is that people couldn't find a way to get back to God on their own. Religion couldn't do it. Rituals and rules couldn't do it. God Himself had to handle the sin problem through the intervention of His Son, Jesus. With His own blood He bought our way back home. He "redeemed" us. Therefore, for everyone who accepts His gift, a brand-new relationship with God takes place. "Therefore, if anyone is in Christ, he is a new creation; the old has gone, the new has come!" (2 Corinthians 5:17) People can become "new again" through a relationship with Jesus.

4. WE HAVE ABUNDANT LIFE WHEN WE OBEY HIM INSTEAD OF LETTING OUR EGOS RULE. Jesus didn't come to lay a bunch of rules on us. He came, as He said in His own words, "that [you] might have life, and that [you] might have it more abundantly" (John 10:10, KJV). Here's an important reality Jesus taught: You can't develop good relationships with people if you don't have a good relationship with God. It just doesn't work. That's why I've taken time to go into all this. What's the use in writing a whole book about people skills if the core problem is left untouched? It's like putting iodine on a swollen finger

with a splinter in it but refusing to take out the splinter! Until you get the splinter out, you can't solve the problem.

People who try to develop people skills without solving the core problem of their own broken relationship with God may appear to make progress. However, they will never get very far in terms of reaching their full potential. Their personal anger, guilt, impatience, and selfishness will eventually sabotage their efforts. You can't solve the basic problem at the heart of human existence by learning good communication techniques. What you've got to do is get yourself a brand-new heart. According to the Bible, this comes through a faith encounter with Jesus Christ.

Be Careful about Judgment

Once you see that people's perspectives about human nature fall into different categories, you run into another dilemma. How do you deal with people who are not on your side of the fence? Maybe you hold a Christian perspective, but what do you do when you encounter people who don't see things that way? Whether it's in your family, your business, or in the world at large, you're going to run into people whose philosophies and lifestyles sometimes radically differ from your own.

Not long ago a young lady friend of mine called asking for advice about an encounter she'd had with a friend from high school. Both of them were now college graduates, and she was interviewing him about a possible business relationship. When she'd known him in school, he was respected, popular, a great student—and after their business discussion, they were both excited about the potential they saw. As they walked to their cars after their conversation, the young man told my friend that he was gay. She was startled by that information.

Personally, she doesn't agree with the morality of that lifestyle. So she told him that, in no uncertain terms.

Sad to say, in the light of that judgment, their business relationship never got off the ground. She called me later on, asking what I thought she should have done. I told her something I think we all need to remember: *Don't ever let your personal judgments destroy the potential in a relationship.* No matter how seriously you disagree with someone else's perspective, deeply respect their right to have it. Treat them with the same kindness and courtesy you desire for yourself. It's important to understand that acceptance is not approval. To be kind to someone is not to condone their lifestyle. It is simply to see them as a person who's precious in the sight of God and to treat them that way.

Remember this: People are not static. They learn. They grow. They can change their minds. But people make positive changes only in an atmosphere of acceptance and love. They will not change in an atmosphere of judgment and condemnation. I can't tell you how many people I've known in my own business who have changed dramatically over the years. One I'm thinking of right now was a motorcycle gang leader. He saw the financial potential in our business right away. But he had no intention of changing his lifestyle, except to add money to it. Because of the kindness and acceptance of his mentors in the business, he developed an ongoing relationship with them that changed his life. Today he's financially free and spends a lot of his personal time teaching young people in high schools what he's learned about building a life that works.

I could tell you dozens of stories like that. After thirty years of working with people in this business, I know one thing for sure: People change. If they're loved, accepted, and given an opportunity to discover truth for themselves, they can change. Whether or not they will is up to them. It's their choice. But it's a sure thing they won't if you cut off the lines of communication before they get a chance.

If you're a Christian, you'll recall that Jesus Himself was criticized by the religious leaders of His day for hanging out with people they didn't approve of. When they asked Him why He did it, He told them, "It's not the well people who need a doctor; it's the sick ones." The reality is we all need to change in some area. In the Bible, the only people Jesus ever criticized were the ones who judged everybody else. So be careful of that. Remember, we're all human. None of us is perfect. We're all learning, growing, and understanding new things every day.

I realize some people think of me as overly opinionated and judgmental. They may have heard me speak on stage about some of the things I believe in—and sometimes I do come down hard on issues I think are important. *But there's a big difference between issues and individuals.*

When I'm talking about issues, whole groups of people who are promoting a certain lifestyle or philosophy, I may say some things that are strongly unfavorable. The fact is, I believe that if certain issues are not dealt with, it could be hazardous to our country and to every individual in it. So I'm not afraid to take a strong stand and voice my convictions in those areas.

But when I'm with people, one-on-one, it's a whole different ball game. Individuals are not issues. They are God's treasures. I don't talk harshly to people. I'm strong about issues, gentle with people. I know from experience that when you're dealing with individuals, acceptance is the foundation, and kindness is the basic skill in creating good relationships.

chapter 10

Emotions and How They Work

In order to become successful and personally effective in relationships, it's important to understand the power of emotions and how to master them—before they master you.

How many times have you heard people say things like this?

- "There's no way I'm going in there to talk to Dave— I've never liked him anyway."
- "I'd like to plan a vacation for next summer, but I'm worried we won't have enough money."
- "I want to get in shape this year, but I never feel like exercising in the morning."

What do these statements have in common? They all reveal the power of emotions. What are emotions, anyway? According to Webster's, an emotion is "a state of feeling... that prepares the body for immediate action."

We like to think we're logical people, basing what we do on sound reasoning and good judgment. But the truth is, emotions influence—and usually dominate—human behavior. As psychologist Dr. Arthur Freeman writes, "Too often common sense deserts us when we most need it and our so-called better judgment is swamped by a tidal wave of emotion."

It's important to realize just how big a role emotions play in our lives. In fact, if you don't understand that, you'll never understand people at all. It's vital to know how emotions work, so you can take control of them instead of letting them take control of you. As you learn the art of mastering your own feelings, your people skills will flourish. But uncontrolled emotions will derail your relationships every time.

Negative Emotions

Feelings always have a charge on them. They're either negative or positive, and it's not hard to recognize which is which. Negative emotions cause you to tense up, to retract on the inside, to move away from people. Positive ones cause you to move toward them. That's why uncontrolled negative emotions will eventually destroy relationships. They have poison in them. And I've discovered that, most of the time, at the bottom of a negative emotion is a lie. Let's look at a few emotions with a negative charge on them.

Fear

Fear tends to be target oriented and specific. It comes from a sense of perceived danger, usually from a specific source. When fear grows, it amplifies your feelings toward a particular object or person. One psychologist calls it "awfulness amplification." When fear is in control, you magnify a specific thing until it grows in your mind to such a proportion that it threatens your emotional equilibrium.

If you allow it to continue, you begin to live with a sense of underlying dread that drains your energy and distorts your thinking. Some people have lived with fear for so many years they don't even recognize it anymore. But it robs them daily of energy and the ability to live life with confidence.

Fear is one of the most common emotions people deal with. God knows so well how dangerous it is that He included over three hundred passages in the Bible where He commanded us to "fear not!" It is not God's will for you to be afraid, because fear is the opposite of trust. In fact, the Bible says that anything apart from faith is sin. So fear is actually sin. When you let fear dominate you, you're missing the mark. "For God did not give us a spirit of timidity, but a spirit of power, of love and of self-discipline" (2 Timothy 1:7).

Worry
Where fear is usually specific, worry tends to generalize. It's brought on by thinking patterns that "catastrophize" things. It starts in the imagination, where you allow fear to drum up possible situations and consequences that bring on anxiety. The truth is, most things you worry about will never take place. But the process of worry itself will drain off your energy and weaken your confidence level. It also gives a negative charge to your personality, repelling other people instead of attracting them.

So what do you do if you're trapped in a worry cycle? Dr. Arthur Freeman suggests three things:

1. When you have a worry-thought, stop and ask yourself, "What made me think this? Why do I have this particular focus in my mind?"

2. Analyze the possible consequences. Ask yourself, "What could logically happen? What will probably happen? Will it be that bad?"

3. Question the evidence. "Is it really correct? How do I know?"

I'm going to add two more suggestions to Dr. Freeman's list:

4. Instead of worrying, formulate a plan and put that plan into action.

5. Trust a loving God. Go to Him in prayer and ask for His help.

Anger

There's a difference between healthy, righteous anger and self-centered anger. When you're angry at injustice or cruelty, it's healthy to get mad. It's actually a positive emotion because it gives you the courage and energy it takes to take action and change things. But selfish anger is something else altogether. Selfish anger occurs when your expectations aren't met. Someone didn't do something your way. Some situation didn't turn out the way you wanted it to, and you're hacked off.

God says man's anger doesn't produce godly results. That's why He says in Ephesians 4:26, "Do not let the sun go down while you are still angry." He knows exactly what self-centered anger can do to us physically, mentally, and spiritually.

Depression

We all go through normal times when we feel "down" because of circumstances, and we know exactly why we're feeling the way we do. At other times we get "down" as a result of physical problems—tiredness, poor health, lack of proper nutrients or vitamins. There are also more serious forms of depression that need professional help.

Professionals tell us there are many different reasons for depression. Sometimes it's a result of unresolved anger that's been repressed over many years and finally becomes depression. Other times it's rooted in boredom—a feeling of purposelessness that occurs when personal dreams and goals are lacking.

If you suffer with depression and can't seem to shake it, it's probably wise to contact a counselor or psychologist for help. They are skilled in tracking down causes and solutions that will get you active in the game of life again.

Hatred

In Matthew 5, Jesus said that if you hate someone, you've committed murder in your heart. Did he mean that you're a criminal, then, and should be punished for that? No. He was making a deeper point that murder always begins with hatred in the heart. Hatred is always an extension of fear or anger. It's a focused intensification of it toward a certain person or group of people—and it is always wrong. The Bible gives no justification for hating anyone. We can hate sin, wrong, and injustice, but we should never hate people. When hate becomes a dominant emotion, it will rip your life apart. Haters cannot win.

Recently I read about a superb hater who hated people with exquisite delight. He was also an alcoholic, had heart trouble, and died in midlife. His story is an example of the poison of hatred in a human life. If someone has hurt or betrayed you and you have nurtured hatred because of that, it's important to handle that situation immediately. The deadly poison of hatred will not harm the individual who hurt you—but it will eventually destroy you.

Forgiveness, as hard as it may seem, is the only antidote for hatred. It doesn't mean that you minimize the damage done by the person who wronged you. It just means that you let go of the pain you're still hanging onto. You trust God to settle the score for you. And you free yourself to go on with your life, without the deadly weight of hatred holding you back.

Everyone experiences negative emotions in life. But when negative emotions become a continual process, a recurring cycle, it's important to find out what's going on. Are you using them unconsciously to gain power over someone? Are they a means for gaining attention or sympathy so that you feel more valuable or important? Are you developing a personality that feeds on these negatives so that people actually see them as part of who you are?

If you're trapped in a cycle of negative emotions that hinders your success and blocks you from the excitement and adventure of life, then it's time to find your way out of the pit and get back into the sunshine that belongs to all of us. Negative emotion, like everything else in life, begins as a decision. Most people don't realize that, so they get tangled up in a web of negativity without ever realizing they chose it in the first place. But the truth is, negative emotions can't hold on to you if you don't hold on to them. You can choose to put them behind you at any point that you become willing to take control of your own thinking. You need to be relentless about your positive thinking. Positive emotions are the ongoing birthright of those who have decided they won't give in to anything else.

Five Positive Emotions
Where negative emotions cause you to retract and back off from relationships, positive ones move you forward into

them. Have you ever wanted something so much, for example, that you got very excited about doing whatever it took to get it? That's a positive emotion. Have you ever felt like you were bursting with happiness and couldn't wait to tell someone about it? That's what positive emotions do. They move us into action and bring us together in constructive relationships. Let's look at a few of the positive emotions that are necessary for success.

Desire
Desire is a hunger for learning, advancement, or improvement of your lot in life in any arena. Desire can be physical, spiritual, mental, or relational. In whatever area desire occurs, it brings with it energy and aliveness. The Bible says, "Hope deferred makes the heart sick, but a longing fulfilled is a tree of life" (Proverbs 13:12).

Confidence
Having confidence means you go through life with a healthy sense of adventure. You have a zest for living, and you enjoy daily challenges. You don't hide out, hoping to escape the normal twists and turns of daily life. Instead, you take them one by one and conquer them. Confidence is a positive emotion about your own ability to deal with life and have it turn out well.

Excitement
Nothing significant is ever accomplished without excitement. Enthusiasm is the surge of emotion that helps you reach your goals. Years ago, Norman Vincent Peale wrote an excellent book called *Enthusiasm Makes the Difference.* His point was that excitement in life is a vital element of success. I've found that to be true. A person without enthusiasm is a person without a dream.

Happiness

Webster's says happiness is "a state of well-being and contentment." It's a positive emotion that stems from the belief that you have access to everything you need that really matters. Unhappy people operate out of a belief that they can't get access to what they need. Over the last thirty years, I've learned that it's up to me to generate what I need in life. God has given me the tools—spiritually and otherwise—to do it. He won't hand it to me on a silver platter because He loves me, and He doesn't want me to be a wimp. He wants me to be strong, like Him. So He gives me the tools and tells me to go out there and get it. Ultimately, there's no one standing in my way but me. Happy people believe that. Unhappy people don't. So happiness or unhappiness boils down to what you believe.

And only you can choose what to believe.

Love

Love means affection, attention, and caring. People today use the word love pretty generically. "I love popcorn," "I loved that movie," or "I love my dog," obviously indicate different kinds of love. But whenever I talk about loving people, I'm talking about the kind of love the Bible says God has—and is. *Agape* is the Greek word for it. It means unselfish, committed love. It's not a passing fancy or a fleeting feeling. It's a decision. A voluntary attitude toward people. It's a positive emotion that operates no matter what the circumstances are.

This kind of love is not naive. It's not based on the innocent belief that people are wonderful and that they'll treat you well. No, this kind of love can go through fire and still be alive, by choice.

I remember when I first got into my own business, I was so excited. I worked hard, I loved the people, and things started growing. I was full of confidence, and in a few months I quit my job to go full-time for myself. I was young and naive. I was in love with life, in love with people, and definitely in love with the opportunity this business had given me to create my own future and help other people create theirs.

It wasn't long till things started happening that changed my thinking. I'm sure they've happened to you, too, if you've been working with people very long. My love affair with people began to take a turn for the worse. I was lied to, again and again. People said they'd meet me at places and didn't show up. I drove hours to keep appointments, only to find the houses empty and dark. Sometimes people wouldn't pay me what they owed me. People I trusted let me down. It was a string of disappointments over a period of time that took my naiveté away from me—and gradually my excitement and energy began to wane.

I didn't really notice what was happening at first. I knew I didn't feel as excited or as confident as I had before. I knew my business wasn't growing like I wanted it to. But I didn't understand why. Finally, it began to dawn on me. I'd let my disappointments steal my dream. I had lost my love for people because they hadn't been how I wanted them to be. They'd disappointed me. Not all of them, of course. There were always the loyal few I could count on. But I had let the disappointments rob me of my love for people. When my naiveté had gone, so had my love. And when my love was gone, so was my enthusiasm, my belief, my hope, and my dream.

It was a big realization for me. I knew I was at a fork in the road. I had to decide what I was going to do. I could not go on with this business without a dream. I could not go on without love. But people were people. They weren't always going to do what I wanted them to do, or be what I wanted them to be. Some of them would hurt me—I'd found that out. The question was this: Would I love them anyway? Suddenly it wasn't about them anymore. It was about me. Did I have the courage to be naive by choice? Not because I didn't know how people were, but because I wanted to believe in them anyway.

Naive by choice. That's what I decided to be. I took back my love, my hope, my belief in people, and I put it back in my heart. Even though I realized people wouldn't always keep their word or operate with integrity or treat me fairly, I would let that be their choice. I would choose to believe in them and to love them—no matter what—because that's who I wanted to be.

That's when my dream came back. One thing I've discovered is that positive emotions are always connected. Negative emotions are connected too. They're like a string of Christmas tree lights. Plug one in, and the rest light up too. When you choose one, you open the door to all the rest of them. Love, for example, opens the way for confidence, hope, enthusiasm, and happiness. Fear brings in worry, anxiety, anger, depression, and hatred. So be careful what doors you are opening in your life.

How Emotions Work

Emotions are connected to thoughts. That's why they can be fleeting or continuous. It depends on your thought patterns. If you think, "I may lose my job and not have enough money to pay the house payment," you'll experience an emotion that is generated by that particular thought. If you think, "I'm trusting God with my finances, and He will show me what to do to succeed," you'll experience a different emotion generated by that thought. If you think a certain thought again and again, you'll generate a thought pattern—which will generate a continuous flow of emotion that goes with it.

One explanation of emotional responses that I've found helpful is this: "Those emotions that bother you, trouble you, or excite you are not stored somewhere deep within, always churning away. Emotions are, in fact, manufactured on the spot as you need them." The Bible says, "As he thinketh in his heart, so is he" (Proverbs 23:7, KJV). Our emotions, as well as our behavior, are determined by our thoughts.

Let's say you got angry with someone at work on Friday. Today is Saturday and you're at the lake, skiing with your family. Do you still feel the emotion of anger? No. When you're not thinking about the situation at work, the emotion disappears. Emotions are manufactured on the spot, as there is need for them.

If you understand how emotions work, it will help you to deal with them more effectively, both in your own life and in other people's. Here are a few things to remember about emotions.

1. EMOTIONS ARE RESPONDERS—NOT INITIATORS. Emotions don't originate thoughts. Thoughts originate emotions. When you experience something, a thought is generated, which in turn produces an emotion. Never let a negative emotion cause you to act without first tracking down the originating thought. Very often, the originating thought of a negative emotion isn't even true.

2. EMOTIONS FOLLOW AN EBB-AND-FLOW PATTERN. Recently I talked with a man who'd lost a loved one. He'd been going through a difficult time and wanted to know if his emotions would ever return to normal. He said his grief seemed to surge in and out, like ocean waves. Just when he

thought he was getting over the pain, it would come over him again. I reassured him that this was normal, and the ebb and flow would continue to happen for a while longer. In times of grief, the surges become less intense and less frequent, until healing finally comes.

This ebb and flow is true of other emotions as well. I've seen it in my business. At seminars, when we all get together, the emotional tide is high. We hear great speakers, we have great thoughts, we experience a corresponding surge of emotion. We're ready to conquer the world. Two or three days later, we're home again, and the emotional tide goes out. But if we listen to some tapes and our thinking gets sparked, we get excited again.

That's the way emotions work. They ebb and flow. It's vital to understand that. Just because you feel something today doesn't mean you will feel it tomorrow. But you can take charge of your emotions by taking charge of your thoughts. As you learn to control your thoughts, you will find you've mastered your emotions too.

3. EMOTIONS HAVE ONLY THE POWER YOU GIVE THEM. What you continually think about is up to you. You're not a victim of your feelings because you're not a victim of your thoughts or your actions. You choose what you think about and what you do.

I can't tell you how many times I've heard grown men tell me, "I can't help it," about lustful emotions that are destroying their integrity and their self-esteem. Yet when I question them, it comes to light that they've been feeding their minds with magazines and other media that promote sensuality. So, of course, their emotions are out of control. But here's the irony: Their thoughts and actions were under their control the whole time. When you realize that, you realize that their emotions are products of their own creation.

The truth is, emotions are very, very powerful. But the only power they have is the power you give them.

4. EMOTIONS CAN BE MISTAKEN. Because what you feel comes from what you're thinking, emotions will be off-base when your thinking is off-base. Imagine this scene. A man needs to borrow his neighbor's lawn mower. He gets up early on Saturday morning, so he won't conflict with his neighbor's schedule. As he's about to walk out the door, he has this thought: "It's too early to go over there. He'll be irritated with me for waking him up. Besides, it's a brand-new lawn mower. I bet he doesn't want anyone borrowing it. I remember one time when I borrowed... " and he remembers a bad experience of borrowing he's had in the past. His mind conjures up thoughts of his neighbor's negative reaction toward him until he's actually getting mad at his neighbor. Finally, he thinks, "I'm not about to ask that jerk for anything. In fact, I'm not going over there anymore, period." For the next week or two, there's tension—and the neighbor has no idea where it came from!

That's why it's so important to keep your thinking on track. Don't let yourself imagine what people will say and do without actually communicating with them and giving them a chance to respond. If you rehearse negative scenarios in your mind, you'll be plagued by a flow of negative emotions, which will eventually crystallize into a negative attitude toward life and toward people.

Mastering Your Emotions

Because emotions are so powerful, it's very important to learn where they come from and how to master them. There are three basic steps to mastering your own emotions:

1. UNDERSTAND THEM. Remember that they don't generate themselves. And they're not stored somewhere waiting to pounce on you unexpectedly. They come from thoughts.

2. ACCEPT THEM. Accepting how you feel doesn't mean you approve of the feeling. It just means you accept the reality of what is going on inside you as a human being. You don't compound the negative energy by getting mad at yourself for feeling the way you do. You acknowledge it, and you check the source to see what thoughts are generating this feeling.

3. CONTROL THEM. Even if you have a powerful emotion going on, you don't have to act on it. You don't ever have to let emotions control you. Instead, you control them by tracking down their source and checking out the truth of the generating thought. Dr. Chris Thurmon, a Christian psychologist, uses what he calls the "TRUTH response" in taking responsibility for your emotions.

> **T** is for the trigger event. What happened that set off the emotion?
>
> **R** is for reflection. Stop a moment and think. What thought or belief is generating this feeling?
>
> **U** is for the unhealthy response. What is it you don't want to do with this emotion?
>
> **T** is for truth. What is the actual truth about this situation?
>
> **H** is for healthy response. Decide what you really want to do to have things turn out for the best.

Next time you find yourself seemingly at the mercy of a negative emotion, give the TRUTH response a try. You'll be amazed at how well it works!

PART Four

Building a Powerful Marriage

Looking for a Life Partner

Life is great—and finding a great partner makes it even better. If you don't have a partner right now, you may be looking for one. If you are, there are some things to understand that will make a big difference in the quality of relationship you create in that arena.

If you're a single adult who's out there building your future on your own, I congratulate you. Your vision and your courage set you apart from the average person, and I want you to know it will pay enormous dividends down the road. But meanwhile, it can be a challenging road. One that you can't help thinking might be better with a partner by your side.

That's why I wanted to make some observations about the dynamics of dating. It's a subject that doesn't apply just to teenagers anymore. Lots of single adults these days are marrying later in life or recovering from lost or damaged relationships and are seriously concerned about how to create a healthy, long-lasting partnership that won't wind up in the ditch again.

Healthy marriage partnerships start with healthy dating relationships. By the time I was seven or eight years old, I already knew I wanted to be married, and I started looking at gals in that light. I went with lots of gals, growing up, and I learned something important from each one of them. In fact, it was during that time that I discovered a lot of the people skills I use today.

The truth is, if you see all of life as a kind of romance, you'll make a lot less mistakes with people. Because it's in the romantic arena that you learn to treat people gently and to see their potential. After all, you have a dream that might be fulfilled with them. It's when you begin to look at possible life partnerships that you suddenly see someone in the light of a dream. That's why this business is like a romance. And if you learn how to succeed at romance, you'll be a long way down the road in understanding how to succeed in business and in life.

Wrong Reasons for Dating

If you have your eyes on the wrong goal, you'll set up patterns that will eventually damage your relationships. There are three motives that will not lead you to happiness and success in your search for a mate.

1. SEX. Our culture has become sex crazy, but that doesn't mean you have to operate like the rest of the world. If you're dating someone in order to just sleep with him or her, it's not a worthy goal, and it'll get you in trouble down the road. We're beginning to see in our society the enormous, negative effects of violating God's laws in this area. In the Bible, God gives specific rules for our own protection. He wants us to have a life that is filled with happiness, so He gives us guidelines that will create that. But too many people are doing their own thing with regard to sexuality.

Even in Christian circles, this is a serious problem. Best-selling author and speaker Josh McDowell has talked about a controversial study that stated that over half of all Christian young men and women from conservative churches had engaged in premarital sex before they were eighteen years old. Sex is definitely an area where the guidelines God sets out are not being understood and observed. That's one reason there's so much emotional wreckage in these young lives.

If you're casual in your attitude toward sex, you're heading for emotional, psychological, and spiritual trouble. This is a wrong goal for any dating relationship. Bodies are not bait; neither are they a toy for you—or anyone else—to play with. I guarantee you, if you'd counseled with as many people as Ron and I have whose relationships are struggling because of all the damage they've done to themselves in this area, you wouldn't be casual about it anymore.

Actually, it's easier to follow God's guidelines of abstaining from premarital sex than to deal with all the consequences. If you've already sinned in this area, then you can still have God's forgiveness and be clean again if you're willing to come to Him in honest faith and trust. Allow Him to forgive you. Stop whatever it is you're doing wrong and get on the right track with God's help. If you've been sexually abused and are still suffering from the aftereffects of that travesty, it's important that you understand how much God loves you and wants to heal your heart. It might be necessary to seek professional help and counseling to help you through that healing process.

2. STATUS. It's insulting to date a person for the sake of how it will make you look. This is the attitude of "I'm more concerned with being seen with you than actually being

with you." That's the mentality of a "user." The status seeker wants to be seen a certain way and uses other people to project that image. He wants to breeze into the office the next day and have people say, "Wow, did I see you with her last night? That's incredible!" It's a way of building your own status by using another person. There's no room in an honorable life for that kind of behavior.

3. SOCIAL PRESSURE. Your friend is going to a party, and she's bugging you to find a date and go too. Or a guy has asked you out, and even though you don't really care for him, you don't want to hurt his feelings and turn him down. So you go out not because you really want to but because you feel you have to. These dates wind up being uncomfortable for everybody. They're not worth the trouble. They devalue the person you're going out with because you're not truly interested in the real person.

You may date because everyone else is doing it. And you don't want to look weird or out of touch. It can even be a matter of pride—you don't want people to think you can't get a date! So you push yourself to go places you don't really want to go with people you don't really want to be with.

When you give in to social pressures, you may not be able to clearly see the other person's potential because you're too preoccupied with what everyone else thinks.

All these motives are shortsighted and self-centered, and they produce nothing of lasting value. I'll tell you what I think the greatest ingredient for a good relationship really is. Contrary to popular opinion, it's not love. I think it's maturity!

Right Reasons for Dating
If you're after the right thing, chances are you'll be looking at the right indicators and wind up with the right kind of

relationship. Here are some healthy reasons for dating someone.

1. TO HONOR GOD. There's a command in the New Testament that says, "So whether you eat or drink or whatever you do, do it all for the glory of God" (1 Corinthians 10:31). What does that mean? Just that we should reflect God's character in everything we do and say. And what does that have to do with dating? A lot, actually. If you'll practice that kind of character when you're in the romantic arena, you'll put yourself in a position to experience a type of relationship you can't have any other way.

I know several people who've told me it helps them to think of Jesus as physically present when they're on a date. It raises the level of everything—from activity to conversation. What's ironic is this: Jesus *is,* in fact, present. So if you act like Him, you're going to experience the power His presence lends to the relationship you're developing.

2. TO BUILD UP THE OTHER PERSON. Sometimes I hear guys say, "I love her because she makes me so happy." Or gals say, "I just love him because he makes me feel so special." Guys, there will be times when she doesn't make you happy. Gals, there will be times down the road when he doesn't make you feel special. Permanent partnerships cannot be based on how the other person makes you feel, or they are destined for disintegration. I think that's a primary reason divorce is so common these days; the partners never got past the selfish motivations for their relationship. So when it quits feeling good, it's all over.

But the best motivation for a long-term relationship is to help the other person become all that he or she can be, to build them up with your love and encouragement and make them greater. If this is your goal, your conversation will be different. You won't talk about yourself so much. You won't try to impress each other. You'll be genuinely interested in the goals and dreams of your partner. You'll want to find out how you can help—how you can encourage and empower them so they can achieve more and go on to dream even bigger dreams.

3. FOR PERSONAL DEVELOPMENT. Relationships are the arena where we grow and develop as people. Opposite-sex relationships give you that opportunity in a special way. You get to learn more about how "the other side" thinks and feels. If you haven't grown up around opposite-sex siblings, you'll learn a lot as you date. And the person you're dating can help you learn a lot about yourself. It's an opportunity to learn to listen more, understand more, and align with someone at a heart level. It's an opportunity to develop loyalty—to become a real friend. The best romantic relationships are built on the foundation of a strong friendship.

4. TO PREPARE FOR MARRIAGE. As you develop healthy relationships, you're laying the foundation for a healthy marriage down the road. It's important that you pay attention when your dating relationships are rocky. The problems you're having may point to a basic flaw in the way you handle yourself. If you have a major problem in the way you look at the opposite sex or the way you treat them, it's good to find this out while you're dating and not after you've said the vows.

Some people have big issues to work out—they were abused as children, or some past trauma has made them suspicious or hostile toward the opposite sex. Dating is an opportunity for discovering areas that need healing before you make a commitment to marriage.

It's important to learn while you're dating how to put someone else ahead of yourself. It's a time of learning about loving sacrifice, compassion, compromise, and caring through bad times as well as good. It's vital to have some real experience with these things before you get into a marriage because a successful marriage will require these skills.

Vital Qualities in the Person You Date

Something also very important to consider is: *What kind of person should I be dating?*

You can have the right motives, but if you're with the wrong kind of person, you still won't wind up with a healthy relationship. All of the following vital qualities should be apparent as you get to know your date. Some personal character traits can be seen from a distance; some you get to know after a time. If any one of these is missing, marriage is out of the question. I'm talking to you the way I'd talk to my own children. Don't take a chance with your life in this area. Be sure that who you're dating has these basic pieces to their personality. If you don't, you'll be paying the price for the rest of your life.

1. RESPECT. Anyone you're dating should always treat you with respect. The reverse is also true—whoever you date should be someone you deeply respect. When a girl told me she was dating a guy against her parents' approval, I asked her why she liked him. "He's so popular at school," she told me. "He's just cool, and everybody likes him." When I asked her how he treated her, she said, "Sometimes he tells me to shut up and bosses me around. But he's popular, and that's what those guys do!" Obviously, this girl's in trouble down the road if she doesn't get rid of this relationship. Her immature values and inability to see what the future holds will cost her dearly.

Respect is the core of all adult love. If you can't respect a person, you can't have an adult give-and-take love relationship. Neither can you develop the deep trust necessary to share your life with someone. Without respect, trust will be shallow, if it's present at all.

2. GOOD MANNERS. You want to date someone who is considerate, thoughtful, and courteous. Sometimes you're attracted to someone with strong charisma, but later you find out they're so powerful they tend to run over other people. It may be exciting to be around this kind of person for a while, but living with them for the rest of your life is another matter.

Common courtesy can help to hold a home together. Simple things like saying "thank you" or "I appreciate that," being considerate of the other person's schedule, and not interrupting when the other person is talking. These are the kinds of things that make it pleasant to be together day after day, year after year.

I've known some guys who think it's manly and macho to dominate other people, especially women. And they become experts at verbally slapping their girlfriends around. What they don't seem to realize is that it's the opposite of manliness to do that. It's actually rude and thoughtless and mean. Gals, if the guy you're dating is like that, you're in for some tough times ahead. I recommend you get off the train tracks before you get run over.

3. EMOTIONAL STABILITY. Who wants to be with someone if you have to walk on eggshells all the time because you might get them upset? Do you want to spend your life with a woman who always pouts when she doesn't get her own way? Or a man who gets angry when he runs into frustration? You don't need a partner who's still an emotional child; you need an adult.

A woman wrote this letter to Dear Abby: "I'm engaged to this guy. He's so unstable that when he doesn't get what he wants, he gets mad and finds the closest thing and kicks it as hard as he can." Dear Abby replied, "Get yourself another guy. Tell him to grow up and quit being a baby, or get somebody else." Real good advice, in my opinion.

It may be amusing to date somebody like that when you're fifteen or sixteen. But if you marry someone who can't control their emotional reactions, you've just created hell on earth. Stability is part of the maturing process, and if one person in a couple doesn't have it, the entire relationship will be out of balance—the stable person catering to the unstable person just to keep things tranquil. Unless you want to become a slave to someone else's emotions for the rest of your life, steer clear of this kind of person.

4. SENSE OF HUMOR. If you can't laugh at life and at yourself, you're in for a long, difficult journey. You always want to date someone who enjoys life and has a healthy sense of humor. (To laugh at other people, by the way, doesn't constitute a sense of humor. Too much of what the world calls humor is actually sarcasm and ridicule.) A real sense of humor is the healthy ability to laugh at yourself and the situations in life that other people take too seriously. It comes from a genuine optimism—a belief that everything will turn out in the end, so you don't have to get too heavy about all the mistakes and frustrations along the way.

A sense of humor gives you resilience. It allows you to get through tough challenges and inconvenient circumstances with a little more bounce in your step. It keeps you from getting too serious when things don't go your way. Over the long haul, it'll keep a marriage going through the tough times, when humorless marriages are getting brittle and falling apart.

5. THINGS IN COMMON. It's important to date someone with whom you can share common values and interests. Although opposites attract to a certain degree, they normally

don't make good partners. Sometimes you enjoy the novelty of someone who's very different from yourself. But the novelty eventually wears off. You're more likely to have a happy, long-term relationship with someone who shares your attitudes and beliefs, your values, and your dreams. The more you have in common, the stronger foundation you can build on, and the more you'll enjoy each other's company.

6. STRONG IDENTITY. There's a strength that comes with knowing who you are and what your purpose is. As far as the Bible is concerned, men are called by God to spiritual leadership in the family. That's why, if you're a woman, you want to date someone who understands where he's going spiritually, professionally, and financially. You want to date a man with strength, but not the kind that is dominating and cruel.

At the same time, you don't want to date someone who lets you dominate him, either. If you do that, you'll find yourself losing your respect for him because you'll eventually realize if he can't stand up *to* you, he can't stand up *for* you either.

Although it hasn't always been culturally acceptable, a woman needs to be strong too. If you're a man, you want a woman who won't back down when it comes to principle and ethics. You want a woman who can work with you to build a dream—and that requires someone with initiative and confidence in who she is and what she can do. Ask yourself, "What will this person be like thirty years from now? Will she stick with me, even be willing to sacrifice if that's what it takes? Or is she someone who has to have everything right now?"

7. BE THE RIGHT KIND OF PERSON YOURSELF. Obviously, if you're going to find the right kind of person, you need to be the right kind of person. It's important to do

an honest evaluation of yourself. Are you the kind of person you would like to date? Do you need to give more attention to your appearance or develop a better sense of humor? Do you know what you believe and why, and do you live by those convictions? Are you flexible and good-natured, even when things aren't going the way you want them to?

If you're a man, do you need to be more of a leader? Do you need to lose some weight or start working out on a consistent basis in order to be more attractive and more physically fit? Do you need to develop your spiritual dimension and clean up the unmanly (and unmannerly) elements of your personality?

If so, then do it. You can, you know. Like everything else, it's a decision. It's up to you to develop the skill to win the kind of person you want for your lifetime mate.

How to Have a Great Date

Most people don't talk about what you should do on a date. Maybe it's considered personal territory, I don't know. But what you do on a date is very important. And if you make your decisions ahead of time, everything is easier. Here are some helpful principles to go by.

1. GUARD YOUR AFFECTIONS. Be careful not to become overly seductive or provocative. Women often don't realize how easily men can be stimulated visually. Many men don't realize that women are easily stimulated through touch. So both of you need to be careful in the way you look and in the way you use physical closeness. Be careful to guard your affections and physical desires. They're precious and valuable. Don't give them away cheaply.

2. PLAN AND ORGANIZE. Have a plan when you meet your date. Know where you're going, what you'll be doing, and how long you'll be there. Be selective about where you go.

If you choose a place where the atmosphere is overly sensual, you're creating a potential for trouble. Also, be selective about who you're with. If you're surrounded by people who are doing things you don't think are right, then their influence can have a negative effect on you.

Don't do the same thing every date—always a movie, always a ball game. You can't learn what the other person is like until you see him or her in a variety of situations. So do a lot of different things together. It doesn't always have to be something fancy or expensive. Simple, everyday things are fun too when you're doing them with someone you really like.

3. GET TO KNOW YOUR DATE'S FAMILY. If you want to know what a woman will be like as a wife, it helps to meet her mother. If you want to know how a man will treat you in the years ahead, notice how he treats his mother now. If it isn't with deep respect and courtesy, beware. That's probably the treatment he'll be giving you down the road when you don't wear a halo anymore.

Ask yourself questions like these: "What values do my date's family have? What's important in their world? What's the atmosphere of their home? What are their beliefs? What are their prejudices? How do they deal with conflict within the family? Do they communicate clearly, or do they cover up feelings until hostility comes out in other ways? Are they supportive or abusive to each other?" Unless there's been radical, life-changing decisions that have altered the direction of a person's life, people tend to turn out a lot like their family did. As you discover the answers to these questions, you'll begin to get a framework that will help you decide if you want to keep dating this person or not.

4. PRAY TOGETHER. As you get to know someone better and better, be sure to develop the spiritual aspect of your relationship. Learn to share your relationship with God. Don't

be afraid to pray together. Study the Bible together and talk about your understanding of the principles you live by. Ron told me he always prayed with his girlfriends at the beginning of their dates. Sometimes they were startled, and sometimes he was a little embarrassed because that's not what everybody usually did on dates. But he determined to do it because it was his goal to be a spiritual leader, and he felt that was the right thing to do.

However you decide to do it, spiritual sharing is a vital part of any potentially long-term relationship. It's not practical to date someone for months or years, finally marry them, and then try to inject spirituality into the relationship. People tend to resist that kind of thing. On your dates you need to be the same kind of person you're going to be as a husband or a wife. You don't want to be one way during your dating relationship and then try to transform (or transform your mate) into another kind of person after the wedding.

You've only got one life to live on earth, and your decisions right now are big decisions. Don't do anything stupid. Do what's right. Have a great time dating. Think of the other person. Have a lot of fun and follow God's principles to protect you. If you follow these guidelines, you'll be able to find your way to a happy marriage and a terrific future.

Keys to a Fulfilling Marriage

One of the relationships that can bring you the most fulfillment and intimacy is marriage. But building a successful marriage requires a powerful combination of two vital elements—commitment and freedom. In a marriage, if you don't have 100 percent of both—you don't have either one.

Not long ago, Ron was with us in Charlotte for a meeting. He got back to his hotel in the early morning hours, around four-thirty. Around six-thirty that morning he was jolted awake by an enormous booming sound that seemed to be almost in the room with him. Since it didn't happen again, he went back to sleep until his alarm went off at 9:30 A.M. As he opened the bathroom door, ready to jump in the shower, he stood in stunned amazement. Ceramic pieces and mud were everywhere. It took him a moment to realize the entire bathroom sink had exploded, like a volcanic eruption, and tree bark and roots were coming out of the place the sink should have been. It seemed impossible, yet he was standing there looking at it. A tree had exploded into his bathroom!

Working around the mess, he managed to take a shower, get dressed, and then he told the clerk, as he checked out, that they needed to check the bathroom of room 111. Apparently there had been a tree root clogged in part of the plumbing, and the pressure had built up until *bam!*— the tree roots broke through!

Communication Blockages

That same pattern happens in relationships. First, there's a clog, a communication blockage. If you ignore it, or work around it, the pressure will build. One day you'll be going about your daily business when *pow!*—your marriage blows up before your eyes. Shocked and puzzled, you wonder what could have gone wrong. What sort of things can clog up your most valuable relationship? Here are a few.

Controlling

Some people are controllers. If you have a habit of needing to be right all the time, of underhandedly manipulating, or of compulsively being the boss in your marriage, you'll eventually run into trouble. It doesn't matter if it's the husband or the wife who's doing it, controlling tendencies are sure to kill your romance as well as other aspects of your relationship. When you control, you smother the other person with your dominance.

Crushing

Other people disregard people they're in a relationship with. They crush the life out of those they love, usually without knowing it. How do you crush the life out of somebody? By ignoring their dreams, their priorities, and the things that are important to them. By putting them down and crushing their self-esteem. No one is so broken as the man or woman who gets no support from a spouse or who gets run over in their partner's pursuit of success. The relationship that should be one of protection is instead full of threats.

Ridiculing

When you're doing it yourself, you usually call it "kidding around." It's a habit people often start out with in marriage. It's the kind of humor that pokes fun at your spouse (or someone else), using their weaknesses or mistakes as an opportunity to laugh at their expense. It's actually another way to crush a person's dignity. And yet when your spouse resists or reacts negatively, you respond with amazement. "I was only kidding. Can't you even take a joke?"

I think it's important to understand something that psychologists have discovered: your subconscious *can't* take a joke. It doesn't know the difference between input that's given in jest and input that's given otherwise. Negative input affects your self-image, whether it was a joke or not. Something happens inside your heart when someone grins and says to you, "You've gained a little weight there, haven't you?" You know they're just kidding. They don't mean to hurt your feelings. But what happens to your self-image, anyway? Suddenly, you're self-conscious, wondering if you really do look fatter than you did last week. Did the fact that they were joking take the sting out of the comment? Absolutely not. Your subconscious accepted it as valid.

In marriage it's vital to protect the dignity of your partner. Think of yourself as the guardian of his or her self-esteem. It's great to have fun together, but whenever you make a personal joke, make sure it's about yourself, not anybody else. I can tell you from experience that the camouflaged insults of misdirected humor can do critical damage to your relationship.

Functionalism

For some people, marriage is just functional. It's a collection of trade-offs. If you're a man, maybe your wife offers you the image you need, and you offer her a paycheck. Maybe it's some other trade-off. But if that's the situation, once you're married, the romance is over because it was just a means to an end, anyway. You see your family as your own private arena of enjoyment, and everyone exists to fulfill the role you've assigned to them. If this fits you, you're in for some big disappointments. If you love the *idea* of the family more than you love the *individuals* in the family, you're going to hit some white water eventually. Your spouse won't fulfill your expectations. Your kids won't either—because they won't want to go by your script. They want you to love them for themselves. They want to be individuals to you—not just players fulfilling their role in your own personal drama.

Negative comparisons

Be careful not to compare your spouse to other people. It's a deathblow to the relationship to wish he were like your father or your brother or your best friend's husband. Likewise, if you compare her cooking to your mother's and her driving to your grandmother's, you're going to pay a high price. The truth is, everyone knows that everyone else is searching for the perfect person. And we all know we don't measure up. We know our weaknesses too well. And if someone we love starts comparing us to other people, it's almost too much to take. It sparks an insecurity that's hard to get rid of. And insecurity can poison a marriage permanently because it strikes at the root of trust that keeps intimacy alive.

I suggest you give up your search for the perfect person and put that energy into improving the one that lives inside of you. Because when you're looking for perfection outside yourself, it's easy to focus on the faults of the one you're married to. Actually, they don't even have to be real faults to become a problem. It can be anything your partner does that doesn't suit you. One psychologist calls them "innocent but annoying habits." An innocent habit will become a horrible turnoff to you if you keep letting your perfection searchlight zero in on it. I recommend you turn off your searchlight altogether and let yourself appreciate the one who had enough wisdom to choose you in the first place! Isn't that perfection enough?

Extracurricular satisfaction

Your deepest heart-hungers should always be met at home by the one who knows you best. This is true spiritually, and it's true in marriage. There's no one outside of God and your spouse who can touch the part of you that's hidden from the world. And if you're trying to fulfill your dissatisfactions in life outside the home—whether it's through alcohol, drugs, extramarital involvements, or whatever else—it won't work. And it will destroy your marriage in the process. It's vital to understand that you can't meet an inside need with an outside substance. Being happy is an inside job. And it's something nobody but you can decide to do.

Lack of responsibility and discipline

It's great to have a good time, but you can't create a good marriage without deciding to grow up. If you're going to be an effective spouse, you're going to have to develop some maturity and the disciplines that successful living requires. Basic principles like hard work, wise priorities, and solid ethics need to become fundamental if your spouse is going to trust you deeply as a life partner. That doesn't mean you don't have fun—far from it! Being disciplined doesn't mean that every minute is scheduled and that you can't ever be spontaneous. It just means that we respect certain principles and keep things in balance.

In fact, discipline actually gives us more freedom than we'd have without it. Just think of the discipline needed to stick to a budget and stay within the solid principles of healthy finances. This is the discipline that frees you from debt. The discipline of loyalty to your spouse in every area is a discipline that grants you a loving life full of trust for each other instead of a shaky relationship that's full of doubt and suspicion.

Inability to accept reality

Relationships are affected when you allow yourself to be driven into depression by the inevitabilities of life. Are you depressed because you have to pay taxes? They have to be paid. Are you depressed by the reality of aging? Aging is a part of life, and you might as well learn to be successful, trust God, and enjoy the ride. Battlefield genius Napoleon Bonaparte made this wise statement: "I do not fight against the inevitables.... Whenever I identify an inevitable that cannot be changed, I always decide not to fight but to turn that inevitable to my maximum advantage."

Why waste your strength fighting something that is unavoidable? Change what you can, and turn what cannot be changed to your maximum advantage. It will build up your mental health and make you a more productive person. Your spouse will be happier with you too because you won't be making war on the world—which also means war at home—anymore.

Living by lies

You can't build a solid foundation on anything but truth. Whether it's a lie in economics, politics, or your personal thinking, you can't build success on it. Whether it's a lie in the bedroom or the boardroom, in your house or the White House, that lie will, piece by piece, tear down the life you've worked so hard to build.

Here are two common lies I've noticed people build on today. The first is that people are dispensable—that they're basically interchangeable parts. It's no wonder that marriages die young when so many people believe that if you're not happy with your wife or husband, you can trade them in for a new one. You just unplug them and plug in somebody else. In that kind of atmosphere, lifelong intimacy can't exist. There's no process of going through all kinds of situations to learn how to be close to one another. The willingness to do that is missing if you see each other as dispensable.

The second lie is equally serious. It's the belief that choices don't have consequences. Actually, the life you're living right now is the result of the choices you've made. Financially, it's true. Relationally, it's true too. The marriage you've got today is what it is because of the way you've chosen to treat each other—whether it's a happy, stable one or a shaky, unfulfilling one. I can tell you this, it's nearly impossible to ignore someone or treat them badly for years and then suddenly clean up your act and save the marriage—because you've been creating the relationship you have day by day according to the kind of person you've been.

Just remember this: Everything you do has consequences. That's why I've taken the time to go over these vital areas where pressure can build up in your marriage. If you take what I've said seriously, later on you'll be glad you did. If you don't, it's like ignoring a crack in the dam. You may be able to overlook it for a while. But the pressure will continue to build up, and when the consequences finally arrive, they're likely to be overwhelming and irreversible.

How to Restore Intimacy

Most marriages cycle through different phases. When you first get married, you're usually in the intimacy stage. But individual perspectives lead to differences of opinion and reaction, even in relationships that are strong and healthy. This inevitably emerges into the conflict stage. Unless you learn how to creatively handle conflict, too often after conflict comes the withdrawal stage.

Nobody wants to end up withdrawn from their wife or husband. So what do we do when we've moved from intimacy into conflict? How can we, instead of withdrawing, move back into intimacy again? Here are a few key principles; let's call them "intimacy injections." In medicine, there are some injections—such as insulin for a diabetic—that have to be given every day for a person to stay healthy. I believe that if we give ourselves daily doses of intimacy, we can keep unhealthy withdrawal from getting the upper hand.

1. RESPECT YOUR PARTNER. Respect begins with kindness and good manners. Life has normal everyday frictions and frustrations, and kindness is the oil that keeps those things from rubbing a relationship raw. Never let yourself become so familiar with your husband or wife that you fail to treat him or her with respect and courtesy. There's never a legitimate reason to be harsh or rude to your spouse, any more than there is to a prospect in your business. No matter what the difficulty or misunderstanding, rudeness only makes the problem worse.

But respect goes deeper than courtesy. Psychologist and author James Dobson says about his wife, Shirley, "I always know my wife is good enough and smart enough to make it without me, on her own. So I'm always winning her, every day." I understand that because I feel that way about my wife, Birdie, too.

Men, you know you've got a really good marriage when you're not the only strong, independent one—when you've helped your wife to become all she can be. You don't want her to be helpless, needing you for everything. You want her to be all right on her own if something happens to you. You want her to be her own person and develop her own gifts and abilities.

It used to be that a woman had to stay with her husband no matter what because most women had no training for the marketplace and relied on their husbands' paychecks. Sad to say, some men not only disrespected them but even treated them badly whenever they felt like it because they knew the women were stuck. Today most women don't have to put up with that kind of treatment from men. And they shouldn't! Real men want real partners, not people who are stuck with us because they're dependent.

One of my favorite Ron-and-Amy stories is the story of what happened on the day after their wedding. It was a happy Kentucky wedding, not far from where they grew up. After the big celebration and an enjoyable wedding night, Ron and Amy were driving around Ron's home-town. Suddenly, Amy said, "Stop the car. I have to get out." Ron thought maybe she was sick, so he pulled into a motel that his uncle owned and said, "Uncle Tom, I need a room." Uncle Tom gave Ron a key and told him to keep the room as long as they needed it. Once they were inside, Amy sat down on the bed and began to sob. When Ron asked her what was wrong and tried to comfort her, she said, "Don't touch me. Don't come near me. I don't even know you. I can't believe I've done this."

It was a frightening experience because both Ron and Amy knew that marriage was a lifetime commitment. Ron felt shocked and rejected. For a frustrated moment, he thought he would just stand up and say, "Hey, enough of this. We're married now. I'm you're husband, you're my wife. This is crazy." Instead, he shot up a prayer for emergency wisdom. Spontaneously, he found himself kneeling in front of Amy, who was still in tears. "Amy, I respect the way you feel, and if you don't want me to touch you, I won't. If you want to go live somewhere else, I'll pay for it. I'll work however many jobs I have to, to do it. But I want you to know I'll always love you. I'll always be committed to you. There'll never be another woman in my life. I will always be married to you, and if we never see each other again, to the day I die, I'll stay committed to you forever." He got up and walked to another part of the room. When he turned around, she was smiling. "I think I'm OK now," she said. "Thank you."

It's not important—although it's not difficult—to understand why Amy got frightened for a moment that day. She and Ron were young. Suddenly she had a new husband and a new life—and she just got scared. But in a moment of supernatural wisdom, Ron knew what he had to do, even in the midst of her rejection, was treat her with respect and tell her he loved her no matter what. He believes *that* moment, not the night before or the wedding ceremony itself, was the beginning of the wonderful intimacy and passion they've had ever since. They've worked at it, of course, and followed these principles to keep that intimacy alive. And they've had it now for over twenty years because of the trust and respect that began at that early—and very crucial—moment.

2. ACT AND SPEAK WITH HONESTY. Without honesty, you don't know what kind of adjustments to make to each other. Psychologist Dr. Willard Harley says, "Honesty is so vital to a relationship because if you're dishonest with your

partner, it's like giving somebody a road map that leads to nowhere. All you do is create frustration." Honesty is required for intimacy. Effective communication won't happen without it.

3. LEAD IN LOVE. Ron says he made a personal commitment early in his marriage to expect everything of himself and nothing of Amy. Most people would say, "That's not fair! Marriage is a fifty-fifty proposition." But that's not the way it works best. If each partner determines to give 100 percent, no matter what, the marriage moves into a powerful dimension it can't operate in otherwise. Ron says his personal 100 percent responsibility commitment has worked miracles in their relationship. "As I expect everything of me, I work harder to create romance, love, and excitement. I stay alert to do the little things I know Amy appreciates. And by expecting nothing from her in return, the biblical law of giving and receiving kicks in. I don't live to get—I live to give. And just like the Bible says, I wind up reaping what I sow. I sow love, and I've reaped in my marriage an incredible response to that love."

Be a love initiator. If you think you'll be taken advantage of, don't worry. It may happen temporarily, but the tide will turn. It's a spiritual law. It has to happen. *If you keep on sowing, you'll eventually reap a harvest beyond your wildest dreams.*

4. PROTECT YOUR SOURCE. What's your source in marriage? Each other. Remember this basic principle: Whenever you're having your needs met by someone, you are preparing to fall in love with that person. That's why a man never lets his secretary do something that only his wife should do for him. A wife shouldn't receive any favor from a boss that the husband should give. You're protecting your source—and your love. Be careful not to let anybody else invade or violate it.

It's important not even to let your own thoughts betray your marriage. I like what Ron calls his internal "thought patrol." He made a commitment years ago to never allow himself to think disparagingly about Amy. Does that mean they never have problems? Of course not. But he relentlessly refuses to allow the poison of criticism to take root in his heart. "I won't let it happen," he told me, "because I'm her lover, her husband, and her best friend. I'm not going to let my own thoughts betray the woman I love." That's protecting your source—even from the negatives that try to sabotage your marriage from the inside.

5. DREAM TOGETHER AND CELEBRATE. One of the most wonderful sources of romance is dreaming in partnership. Working together in business can be fantastic when you trust each other and are both taking part in making your dreams happen. You might call it "dream blending" because it ends up being more than what either one of you would have created alone. When you blend your dreams, excitement grows in all areas of your life together.

And when you know you're building a dream together, you have a constant cause to celebrate. I don't mean just rewarding yourself for an accomplishment, either. That's good. But celebration goes beyond that. It's important to just have fun with each other. All of us need fun and celebration in our lives. And it doesn't always have to cost money. If you don't think you have time for fun, you don't understand the power of it in your relationship. Once you realize that, you'll make the time. I don't know anybody much busier than Birdie and I, but we purposely make time to have fun together. We're best friends, and having fun is an important part of that.

6. MAKE SEX A PRIORITY. In Proverbs 5:18–19 the Bible says, "May you rejoice in the wife of your youth....

May her breasts satisfy you always, may you ever be captivated by her love." Those words are sexual words in Hebrew. It's important to know and understand that God's the author of sexuality. He's not against it; He made it up! The only kind of sex He opposes is the kind that is outside of a marriage commitment. But sex as a married couple is an incredible bond. It's a wonderful intimacy. And the most successful sex act is the joyful passion between a man and his wife committed to each other for life in a happy marriage. There's nothing to compare to that, if you're willing to work for it.

If your relationship is troubled by some kind of sexual problem, there are resources to help you. Maybe one of you feels withdrawn or inhibited, or perhaps there's a physical problem. See your doctor or a counselor to get some honest input. Ed Wheat has written a wonderful book, *Intended for Pleasure,* that might give you some insight into your situation. The point is, get the help you need. Don't miss out on this wonderful dimension of marriage.

Dr. Harley said that when he was a young psychologist, he'd try to help people with their marriage problems, but very often they would end in divorce in spite of what he did. Then he began to concentrate on helping the couples with their sex life. After that, his success rate skyrocketed. It seemed these married couples began to enjoy their sexual relationship so much they actually wanted to stay together—and they got more willing to work on the other aspects of the relationship. This may sound like the opposite of what I've said about intimacy coming before sexuality—but in marriage, if you "lose the spark," sometimes it's important to regain that aspect of your relationship before you can work out the other things. Because, while sex certainly isn't everything, it's a lot. And those who minimize it are missing one of the strongest intimacy injections in life.

7. BE UNITED SPIRITUALLY. My deepest unity with Birdie has come through our individual and shared relationship with Jesus. His forgiveness, His power, and His presence with us every day have transformed our marriage and brought us to a unity we could never have approached simply on human terms. A spiritual unity is the greatest unity of all. It's worth every principle we've followed. It's the sweetest experience you can know.

As you grow in your skills with people, you're going to have not just a great business but a great marriage and a great life. As you protect your marriage with solid principles and you master the secrets of true, committed intimacy, you'll enjoy the amazing freedom and fulfillment God designed marriage to be.

You *Can* Do It!

Do you know what dogged determination is? It's getting a heart grip on something and refusing to let go until you've mastered it. I've heard about Albert Castel, now a famous Civil War historian, who's written one of the most respected books, ever, on the Atlanta campaign of 1864. He said his passion for the Civil War era began when he was thirteen years old and went to see *Gone with the Wind.* "When I left the theater four hours later," he writes, "I was in love with *Gone with the Wind.* Saturday morning I began to read the novel... by Friday I had finished, whereupon I saw the movie again at the same theater. Love is a glutton that craves whatever will feed it. Since the pivotal historical event of *Gone with the Wind* is the Atlanta campaign, I checked out the fourth volume of *Battles and Leaders of the Civil War....* I perused most of the rest of that volume and the preceding three.... For my fourteenth birthday I asked my parents to give me, and I got, the recently published first volume of *Lee's Lieutenants.* After reading this book and Freeman's four-volume *Robert E. Lee,* I devoured everything else I could get my hands on pertaining to the Civil War."

Now that's a man with a passion. It's no wonder he's a big winner—he had that dogged determination to learn all he could about what had become a priority in his life. And you can develop that kind of determination in your relationships, too. Because, frankly, there's nothing more pivotal to your success or failure in life than your personal relationships.

There are many stories like that about people with dogged determination who never give up in their pursuit of excellence. When B. C. Forbes, founder of *Forbes* magazine, was only fourteen, he was doing jobs he hated. But he also wrote, "So what! It will get me closer to my goal to go to America from Scotland!" He was doggedly determined to do whatever it took, even if he hated the process, to get him to his goal. That's the attitude a winner always has.

Charles Schwabb worked for the Carnegie steelworks in Pennsylvania. Bill Jones was his foreman, and he had the chief draftsman inform the men under him that they had to put in overtime without pay for a special project. Those who worked with enthusiasm and without complaint were to be recommended to Jones for future advancement. Charles Schwabb was the only name on the list. It's no wonder he became one of the most famous entrepreneurs of his generation. Dogged determination in keeping your attitude right is a vital element of success, both in relationships and in all of life.

Jack Stack is head of an organization called Springfield Remanufacturing Corporation. Years ago he worked for another company that had to bring in steel for their production. But at that time, there was a violent steel strike going on at the U.S. steel plant. Without steel, the production line was paralyzed. What to do? They got together and came up with a plan. They figured if they hired school buses to go in and pick up the steel and had the bus drivers dress up like nuns, they could get them through the strikers' line without being threatened or shot. Sure enough, the plan worked. Jack Stack observed later, "It was incredible to have that kind of experience, knowing there was a way to win and we were going to find it. We were so determined to get the job done that we decided nothing was going to stop us." That's how a winner thinks. It's the spirit of dogged determination.

Now, what about you? Are you passionately determined to succeed in your life and relationships? Or are you going to fall apart when somebody criticizes you? Are you going to give up when the winds of opposition come against you? Dogged determination is the true mark of a winner.

May God bless you as you begin to put your game plan into practice. Just remember, always, to believe in yourself. Get your principles right. Be determined to love people no matter what. Then set your sights on the dream—and never give up.

I love you.

Dexter

EPILOGUE
by Doyle Yager

The true test of a man is not his words, but his life.

Dexter and Birdie have the ability to make each person they're dealing with feel like they have a special place in their heart that nobody else can fill. Especially Dex, when he's talking he makes you feel like you're the only person in the room. It's an amazing ability, and I've seen it operate whether he's dealing with an individual or a couple. Even when he's talking to a coliseum of thousands, you feel that he's actually talking to you! I watch both Dex and Birdie carefully whenever I can, to see how they do it, because that's what people need. And I think when we all learn to do that, we will change this world.

—Cherry Meadows

I've always heard my dad say, success is the progressive realization of a worthwhile dream—and learning to love people is the most important part of success. Our prayer for you is that you will master, progressively, the skills and attitudes that empower people to become all they can be. You can't do it in a day, or a week, or a year. But every day you can do it a little more, a little better than you did the day before.

Greatness comes in small, bite-sized pieces, one day at a time. In fact, it's the little things that make up the big things in life. Dexter didn't learn all he's learned in a day—and he didn't become what he's become because of the big events and big people he's encountered. He learned it in small doses, day to day, month by month, year by year, over the 50-plus years he's been alive.

I wish I could have included in this book all the letters and comments that came to me from people who've experienced Dexter personally. They're like puzzle pieces... small pictures that, together, make up the whole. Perhaps, someday, we'll publish a companion volume to this book that is made up of nothing but those individual stories. Each one is a little window into the heart, mind, and soul of a man whose understanding has changed the lives of so many.

One thing we have each discovered about Dexter is this: Even though he's unique, parts of him can be totally duplicated. That's why he shares what he knows so tirelessly. Dexter is fully aware that anyone who's willing to follow the pattern and do what he's done, acting on the principles he's discovered, will get the same results he's gotten. That's why he wanted to share them with you. He wants you to have every bit of the joy, love, and success your heart desires. It's available. You just have to learn the way—one day at a time.

Let me close this book with a scene I believe expresses the heart of my father as well as any I've heard. As a matter of fact, I've watched this very scene myself many times. It expresses the tireless tenacity of a man who cares about people—not just with his words but with his life. May God bless you with the same measure of love—and success—in your own life.

During the mid to late '70s, when major functions were held in the old Charlotte Coliseum, I used to see an example of giving and serving by Dexter that became his trademark and a standard all of us could strive to duplicate.

Then, even more than now, Saturday's marathon session usually ended somewhere between 2 and 4 A.M. Dexter would then stand on stage for hours, shaking hands, hugging and encouraging any and all who would line up to wait. Some brought questions, others greetings, but mostly they just wanted to touch "the man." They wanted to look into those dancing eyes and get an encouraging word.

I can remember finishing up a "night owl" session of my own in one of the corners of the Coliseum and seeing Dex still standing on stage with a line of hopefuls stretching halfway around the Coliseum floor. I left to catch an hour or two of sleep before I had to be back for a meeting with the leaders who met before the worship service on Sunday morning.

When I returned for the meeting, the sun had just come up. (It looked redder than usual through my bloodshot, sleep-deprived eyes.) As I reentered the Coliseum, there was Dexter, on stage, still greeting and encouraging—just finishing up the end of the line of the faithful who had waited their turn for their moment with him.

Dex, being the consummate giver, always said to the leaders just before a function, "You can sleep on Tuesday." That's when you've given as much as you can, to as many as you can, for as long as you can. The hungry have been filled. The shepherd has fed his sheep.

—Roland Hughes

PART ONE: DEVELOPING DYNAMIC RELATIONSHIPS

I. Situations Change When You Change *3*
  A. Growing Up *4*
  B. Characteristics of an Immature Person *6*
    1. Living in the immediate *6*
    2. Short on discipline *6*
    3. Dominated by emotions 7
    4. Limited knowledge without knowledge of the limits 7
    5. Operating from a sentimentality base, not a reality base 7
    6. Sexually absorbed *8*
    7. Identity sensitive *8*
  C. Ten Obstacles to Personal Change *8*
    1. Get rid of the "positive cover" *9*
    2. Avoid the "hidden hooks" of life *9*
    3. Let go of your "comfort blanket" *11*
    4. Give up deceptive desires *12*
    5. Quit being suspicious of change *12*
    6. Spring the trap of small thinking *13*
    7. Don't ignore the passing of time *13*
    8. Avoid fantasy-filled failure *14*

9. Destroy lethal laziness before it destroys you *14*

10. Quit sabotaging yourself by focusing on yourself *15*

D. A Responsible Maturity *16*

II. Positive Patterns for Success *21*

A. Nailing Down the Nonnegotiables *21*

B. Personal Nonnegotiables *22*

   1. Health *22*

   2. Family and friends *22*

   3. Morality *23*

   4. Spiritual life *23*

C. Sticking to Your Nonnegotiables *24*

D. Developing Principles for Successful Living *25*

   1. *Behavior builders* *25*

      a. Make friends with the realities of life *26*

      b. Take responsibility for your actions—and your reactions *26*

      c. Choose inspiring role models *26*

      d. Get excited by the possibilities *27*

      e. Get a direction and a mission *27*

      f. Practice forgiveness *28*

      g. Maintain sensible security *29*

      h. Balance time with people and time alone *29*

      i. Live in obedience to God *30*

   2. *Productivity guidelines* *30*

      a. Know and control your aggravation scale *30*

      b. Be willing to stretch *31*

      c. Ride the emotional flow of your life *32*

      d. Declare war on personal weakness *32*

      e. Keep your promises *33*

E. The Secret of a Superperformer *34*

III. Moving Forward with People   *35*
    A. Twenty-One Dynamic People Skills   *35*
        1. Practice a friendly flexibility   *36*
        2. Broadcast positive body language   *36*
        3. Keep your voice pleasant   *38*
        4. Express convictions appropriately   *38*
        5. Listen attentively   *39*
        6. Be prepared   *40*
        7. Be authentic   *41*
        8. Find a connection   *41*
        9. Build bridges   *42*
        10. Be empathetic   *43*
        11. Stand firm   *44*
        12. Defuse conflict   *44*
        13. Focus on a solution   *45*
        14. Use a "can you help me?" approach   *48*
        15. Practice the "duck response"   *48*
        16. Develop a sense of humor   *48*
        17. Express genuine praise and appreciation   *49*
        18. Exude happiness   *50*
        19. Make change easy   *50*
        20. Become a storyteller   *50*
        21. Pray with and for people   *51*
    B. Loving People   *51*

IV. How to Stay Motivated Forever   *53*
    A. What Motivates People?   *53*
        1. *Desire for respect*   *53*
        2. *A sense of legacy*   *54*
        3. *Need for financial security*   *54*
    B. The Pursuit of Pleasure   *55*
        1. *Unreached goals of childhood*   *55*
        2. *Desire for power*   *56*

     3. *Desire for good health*   *56*
     4. *Desire to please God*   *56*
     5. *Helping others*   *57*
     6. *The joy of life itself*   *57*
  C. Motivation Murders   *58*
     1. *Withdrawal from relationships*   *58*
     2. *Loss of energy*   *59*
     3. *Moral muck*   *59*
     4. *Surrendering to doubt*   *59*
     5. *Trying to be somebody else*   *61*
     6. *Gorillas from the past*   *61*
     7. *Laziness and pessimism*   *62*
     8. *Guilt*   *62*
  D. Staying Motivated   *63*
     1. *Focus on your dream*   *63*
     2. *Remember who you influence*   *63*
     3. *Remember honor and duty*   *63*
     4. *Keep good role models in front of you*   *64*
     5. *Get your daily surge*   *64*
     6. *Just do it!*   *64*

PART TWO: KNOCKING OUT NEGATIVES THAT
SPOIL YOUR RELATIONSHIPS

V. Deal with Regret   *69*
  A. Sources of Regret   *69*
     1. Emotional baggage   *70*
     2. Halfheartedness   *71*
     3. Deliberately hurting someone   *71*
     4. Missed opportunities   *72*
     5. Not taking care of yourself   *72*
     6. Financial missteps   *72*
     7. Relationship blunders   *72*

        8. Unfulfilled personal expectations   *73*

   B. Why It's Hard to Deal with Regret   *73*

        1. Fear of personal guilt   *73*

        2. Fear of ongoing damage   *74*

        3. Fear of emotional exhaustion   *74*

        4. Powerless depression   *74*

        5. Spontaneous anger   *74*

   C. How to Handle Regret   *75*

        1. Make a clean sweep   *75*

        2. Commit to a forward focus   *75*

        3. Be your own best friend   *76*

        4. Develop a disciplined memory   *76*

        5. Practice thankfulness   *76*

        6. Get a strong dose of "so what?"   *76*

        7. Concentrate on giving   *77*

        8. Acknowledge a spiritual base   *77*

        9. Believe in yourself   *78*

   D. Turning Your Life Around   *78*

VI. Overcome Rejection   *81*

   A. Seven Reasons People Reject You   *82*

        1. You've become a threat to their lack of
           performance   *82*

        2. Jealousy   *83*

        3. Reluctance to change   *83*

        4. Misconceptions   *84*

        5. Mistrust   *84*

        6. Dislike   *84*

        7. Experiences of personal rejection and
           disappointment   *85*

   B. How Rejection Affects You   *85*

        1. It causes you to doubt your judgment   *86*

2. It challenges relationships you thought were secure *86*

3. It feeds your natural insecurity *87*

4. It cracks your confidence *87*

5. It attacks your most basic motivation *88*

C. How *Not* to Respond to Rejection *89*

1. Rapid retreat *89*

2. Sellout to self-doubt *90*

3. Camouflaged compromise *90*

4. Approval pursuit *91*

5. Becoming a turtle *91*

6. Recycling the rejection *91*

7. Rejection reflection *91*

D. Right Ways to Respond to Rejection *92*

1. Spiritual clarity *92*

2. Battle training *92*

3. A love of excellence *93*

4. True grit *92*

VII. Get a Grip on Your Ego *95*

A. How's Your Ego Doing? *95*

1. You feel secretly hurt or resentful when other people are recognized or rewarded *96*

2. You tend to resist new information *96*

3. You talk about yourself too much *97*

4. You tend to de-edify other people *98*

5. You resist constructive feedback *98*

6. You treat the laws of God lightly *99*

B. How to Retain Humility *100*

1. Never lose your sense of wonder at what you're learning from others *100*

2. Cultivate gratefulness *100*

3. Pray for a giving attitude *100*

4. Make people your priority   *101*
5. Learn to see yourself from God's perspective
   101

VIII. Eliminate Negative Patterns   *103*
    A. Negative Relationship Patterns   *103*
        1. *Temperamentalism   103*
        2. *Response laziness   104*
        3. *Reaction ruts   105*
        4. *Relational fantasies   106*
        5. *Operating from assumptions, not facts   107*
        6. *Pouring negatives onto others   108*
        7. *Manipulation games   109*
        8. *Attack of the raptor   109*
    B. Changing Negative Patterns   *110*
        1. *Don't be trapped by perfectionism   111*
        2. *Don't ignore your vulnerabilities   111*
        3. *One other thing to avoid   113*
    C. Turning Negative Patterns into Positive Ones   *113*

PART THREE: UNDERSTANDING WHO
YOU ARE

IX. Choosing Your View of Human Nature   *117*
    A. The Humanistic View of People   *118*
        1. Life is primarily a physical phenomenon   *118*
        2. People are simply an advanced form of animal
           life   *119*
        3. People are morally neutral   *119*
        4. People are environmentally controlled and
           developed   *120*
        5. People are naturally capable of unlimited
           improvement   *120*

B. The Christian View of People *121*
  1. People are created in God's image *121*
  2. We're a flawed creation *121*
  3. God made recovery possible *122*
  4. We have abundant life when we obey Him instead of letting our egos rule *122*
C. Be Careful about Judgment *123*

X. Emotions and How They Work *127*
  A. Negative Emotions *128*
    1. *Fear* *128*
    2. *Worry* *129*
    3. *Depression* *130*
    4. *Anger* *130*
    5. *Hatred* *131*
  B. Five Positive Emotions *132*
    1. *Desire* *133*
    2. *Confidence* *133*
    3. *Excitement* *133*
    4. *Happiness* *134*
    5. *Love* *134*
  C. How Emotions Work *136*
    1. Emotions are responders—not initiators *137*
    2. Emotions follow an ebb-and-flow pattern *137*
    3. Emotions have only the power you give them *138*
    4. Emotions can be mistaken *139*
  D. Mastering Your Emotions *139*
    1. Understand them *140*
    2. Accept them *140*
    3. Control them *140*

PART FOUR: BUILDING A POWERFUL MARRIAGE

XI. Looking for a Life Partner   *143*
   A. Wrong Reasons for Dating   *144*
      1. Sex   *144*
      2. Status   *145*
      3. Social pressure   *146*
   B. Right Reasons for Dating   *146*
      1. To honor God   *147*
      2. To build up the other person   *147*
      3. For personal development   *148*
      4. To prepare for marriage   *148*
   C. Vital Qualities in the Person You Date   *149*
      1. Respect   *149*
      2. Good manners   *150*
      3. Emotional stability   *150*
      4. Sense of humor   *151*
      5. Things in common   *151*
      6. Strong identity   *152*
      7. Be the right kind of person yourself   *152*
   D. How to Have a Great Date   *153*
      1. Guard your affections   *153*
      2. Plan and organize   *153*
      3. Get to know your date's family   *154*
      4. Pray together   *154*

XII. Keys to a Fulfilling Marriage   *157*
   A. Communication Blockages   *158*
      1. *Controlling*   *158*
      2. *Crushing*   *158*
      3. *Ridiculing*   *159*
      4. *Functionalism*   *160*
      5. *Negative comparisons*   *160*
      6. *Extracurricular satisfaction*   *161*

7. *Lack of responsibility and discipline* 161

8. *Inability to accept reality* 162

9. *Living by lies* 162

B. How to Restore Intimacy 164

   1. Respect your partner 164

   2. Act and speak with honesty 166

   3. Lead in love 167

   4. Protect your source 167

   5. Dream together and celebrate 168

   6. Make sex a priority 168

   7. Be united spiritually 170